FITTING IN
A Functional/Notional Text for Learners of English

MARGARET POGEMILLER COFFEY
Donnelly College

PRENTICE-HALL, INC., Englewood Cliffs, New Jersey 07632

Library of Congress Cataloging in Publication Data

COFFEY, MARGARET POCEMILLER.
. Fitting in.

1. English language—Text-books for foreigners.
I. Title.
PE1128.C67 1983 428.2'4 82-16501
ISBN 0-13-320820-6

Editorial/production supervision and
interior design: F. Hubert
Page layout: Jill Packer
Cover design: Karolina Harris
Manufacturing buyer: Harry P. Baisley

This book is dedicated to my husband, Tom.

Printed in the United States of America

10 9 8 7 6 5 4 3 2 1

ISBN 0-13-320820-6

PRENTICE-HALL INTERNATIONAL, INC., *London*
PRENTICE-HALL OF AUSTRALIA PTY. LIMITED, *Sydney*
EDITORA PRENTICE-HALL DO BRASIL, LTDA., *Rio de Janeiro*
PRENTICE-HALL CANADA INC., *Toronto*
PRENTICE-HALL OF INDIA PRIVATE LIMITED, *New Delhi*
PRENTICE-HALL OF JAPAN, INC., *Tokyo*
PRENTICE-HALL OF SOUTHEAST ASIA PTE. LTD., *Singapore*
WHITEHALL BOOKS LIMITED, *Wellington, New Zealand*

CONTENTS

TO THE TEACHER

The goal of *Fitting In* is to teach certain functions of English to English-language learners. It is intended for high-beginning/low-intermediate students in preacademic programs *and* intermediate/advanced students in adult programs.

Fitting In is student-centered. With a minimum of teacher explanation, students can quickly begin to produce meaningful language in a variety of situations.

Several different exercises have been developed to teach each function. This provides students with ample opportunity to reinforce the newly learned structures while maintaining a high level of interest.

Students are first presented with the language of a particular function. When appropriate, this language is presented with a scale of formality which contrasts the function's formal and informal expressions. These expressions are then reinforced in a variety of exercises. At the beginning of each lesson, exercises are very controlled. As the lesson progresses, exercises become increasingly unstructured. The chapter concludes with a review exercise and an exercise in which students are expected to supply most of the verbal and nonverbal language themselves.

ACTIVITIES IN EACH CHAPTER

1. *For a Better Understanding.* This is the only part of the book in which a language function is directly explained. This section deals with certain aspects of the use of a function which are taken for granted by native English speakers, but which may be unfamiliar to the ESL learner. I have tried to cover points which, if not understood correctly, could lead to embarrassment, frustration, or confusion on the part of the language learner.

2. *Conversation Practice with a Friend.* In this exercise students are given several conversation situations. The first two conversations are completely written out. In the others, basic information is given from which the students create their own conversations. Students practice these dialogues in pairs (or groups of three) and concentrate on structure, accuracy, pronunciation, and intonation.

3. *Role Plays.* There are many types of role plays throughout the book. Some are nonverbal role plays, others are short conversations which can be quickly completed, and still others are lengthy role plays that require a great deal of preparation. The goal of the role plays is to create a realistic environment in which students are encouraged to use props and nonverbal gestures. They are also encouraged to present their conversations rather than read them.

4. *Community Exercises.* These exercises are designed to allow students to use in the community the functions they have learned in the classroom. Through these exercises, students talk and listen to English-language speakers, watch T.V., read street signs, and so on. The goal of these community activities is to give students confidence to use these English structures on their own.

SUPPLEMENTAL ACTIVITIES

1. *Rotation Activities.* These activities are meant to be a "fun" way to reinforce the structures of certain functions. In some activities there is a key position (the person who is "it") which rotates several times throughout the exercise. In others, each student is given an assignment which he or she is asked to complete by questioning several other students. The students "rotate" in that they are constantly moving about the classroom interacting with each other. These activities are designed so that the teacher does not have to participate. This gives the teacher the freedom to circulate among the different groups while the exercise is in progress.

2. *What Would You Say?* and *Thinking on Your Feet.* These exercises present students with an opportunity to assess a given situation and respond to it appropriately. "What Would You Say?" is a written exercise. In some instances, students write parallel dialogues which directly contrast the formal and informal expressions of a function. In others, students are furnished with an incomplete conversation or situation which covers a certain function. They are asked to identify the function and reply in an appropriate manner. "Thinking on Your Feet" is an oral exercise; however, it is very similar to "What Would You Say?" Both groups of exercises could easily be modified and presented as either written or oral lessons.

3. *Mix and Match.* Many of the "Mix and Match" activities are traditional in that students are asked to match a question in one column with an appropriate response in the other. In some of these activities, however, pairs of students "mix and match" given information to create original conversations.

4. *One-Sided Dialogues.* These are incomplete dialogues in which only one person's lines are given. Based on cues from the given lines, students are expected to complete the missing portion of the dialogue. The finished dialogues can then be practiced in pairs.

5. *Choose the Dialogue.* This activity contains two complete dialogues. After the first student reads an opening line, the second student has a choice of replies. The reply he or she makes dictates the course of the remainder of the dialogue. This activity forces students to carefully listen to each other.

6. *Problem-Solving Activities* and *Discussion Activities.* The functions towards the end of the book are such that they need to be practiced in a discussion format. These activities give students an opportunity to actively engage in conversation with partners, within small groups, or with the entire class.

WORKING THROUGH A CHAPTER

It might be helpful to outline one possible way to work through a chapter.

1. *Presenting the Function.* Students are initially presented with a chart outlining the language of a particular function. Immediately following the chart is "For a Better Understanding." It is recommended that these two sections be introduced together as they are intended to help students become familiar with the language of a function before using it. The chart provides a format for students to practice the pronunciation and intonation of the language expressions. It also gives teachers the opportunity to introduce the formality and informality of the different expressions. Using "For a Better Understanding" as a starting point, teachers can discuss potentially unfamiliar uses of the function which could embarrass, frustrate, or confuse the language learner.

The amount of time spent presenting a particular function will, of course, depend on the needs of the students. It is suggested, however, that teachers move through these two sections as quickly as possible. They are meant to be a reference point for students as they practice the function throughout the remainder of the chapter.

2. *Practicing the Function.* After students are introduced to a function, they are asked to practice it in "Conversation Practice with a Friend." In this activity students are given the necessary information from which they can create their own conversations.

There are many ways to practice these situations. Some teachers may want to pair up students and have everyone practice the conversations at the same time. Others may want to ask two students to present a conversation to the entire class. By having people work in pairs or small groups, the teacher has a chance to circulate and help individual students with structure, pronunciation, intonation, and new vocabulary.

This activity is intentionally designed so that students with different levels of ability can benefit from it. Some students will prefer to only practice the function being introduced, much like the two examples at the beginning of "Conversation Practice with a Friend." Others will want to expand on the information given and create a more comprehensive and unrestricted conversation.

Pairing students of similar levels is beneficial. Weaker students feel successful creating brief conversations while stronger students have the opportunity to learn from each other by going beyond the assigned activity. It is also useful to sometimes pair weak and strong students together. Slower students can definitely benefit from this situation and strong students can improve by helping other classmates.

3. *Using the Function.* Following "Conversation Practice with a Friend" students are presented with two types of activities in which they "use" the function just learned. The first kind of exercise, described on the preceding pages, is used in the classroom. The actual activities vary from chapter to chapter. Depending on the needs of the students and class time constraints, a teacher may want to use all, a few, or in some cases none of these reinforcement activities.

The second type of activity, "Community Exercises," is designed to be used outside of the classroom in the community. To gain the most benefit from them, it is suggested that the community activities first be introduced in class by the teacher. Then the students can do the activity on their own. Finally, it is a good idea to have a follow-up discussion in which students present the results of their community experience to the others. This step-by-step approach emphasizes the importance of this activity even though it is done outside of an actual classroom.*

4. *Reviewing the Function.* At the end of the chapter is a section entitled "Putting It Together." In this section, students have an opportunity to review all the functions they have learned. They are first presented with one of a variety of activities to be used in or out of the classroom. They are then given several role plays to be acted out in class. It is recommended that special attention be given to these final role plays. They are intended to be the culmination of the students' learning experience in which they create meaningful language in a realistic environment using as many props and nonverbal gestures as possible.

ACKNOWLEDGMENTS

I wish to extend my sincere thanks to Dr. Steven J. Molinsky of Boston University. His inspiration and guidance were instrumental in the creation of this text.

*Numbers 1, 2, and 3 are repeated for each function presented in a chapter.

CHAPTER 1

INTRODUCTIONS

- Introducing Others
- Forms of Address
- Introducing Yourself
- Nonverbal Introductions
- Making Small Talk After Introductions

Introducing Others

You can introduce people by saying:

It's my pleasure to introduce *Frank Brown.**	↑ formal
Mrs. Johnson, I'd like to introduce *Mr. Brown.*	
Mrs. Johnson, I'd like you to meet *Mr. Brown.*	
Patty, this is *Frank.*	
Patty, have you met *Frank?*	
Patty, do you know *Frank?*	informal ↓

Some replies:

How do you do?	↑ formal
(It's a) pleasure to meet you.	
(It's) nice to meet you.	
(I'm) glad to meet you.	
(I'm) happy to meet you.	
Hello.	
Hi.	informal ↓

* This expression is generally used to introduce one person to a group of people.

Forms of Address

Here are some of the common titles used in English. Discuss the meaning of each one with your teacher.

Mr. Brown	Professor ______	Reverend ______
Mrs. ______	Dr. ______	Judge ______
Miss ______	Father ______	Officer ______
Ms. ______	Rabbi ______	

When making a *formal* introduction in English, the introducer often uses the people's titles and family names. For example:

Person A: *Ms. Winston,* I'd like you to meet *Dr. Thomas.*

Person B: It's nice to meet you, *Dr. Thomas.*

Person C: It's nice to meet you, too, *Ms. Winston.* *

*If someone introduces you by your last name (Dr. Thomas), but you would like to be called by your first name (Joe), you can say: Please call me Joe.

When making an *informal* introduction in English, the introducer generally uses the people's first names. Sometimes first and last names are used. For example:

Person A: *Martha,* I'd like you to meet *Joe (Kaplan). Joe,* this is *Martha (Stone).*

Person B: Nice to meet you, *Joe.*

Person C: Happy to meet you, too, *Martha.*

In some very informal situations, the introducer may use only the people's names. For example:

Person A: *Bob,* *Tom.*
Tom, *Bob.*

Person B: Hello *Tom.*

Person C: Hi *Bob.*

FOR A BETTER UNDERSTANDING

Sometimes when you are making introductions problems occur because you may call the person by one name (Mom, Dad, Kim . . .) but need to introduce him or her by another (Mrs. Harrison, Mr. Harrison, Dr. Turner . . .). For example, how do you avoid the following situation when introducing your mother to one of your teachers?

Person A: *Mom*, I'd like you to meet *Dr. Gibson.*

Person B: It's a pleasure to meet you, *Dr. Gibson.*

Person C: It's nice to meet you, too, *Mom!?!*

To avoid this situation make two complete introductions. Look at the following example:

Person A: *Mom*, I'd like you to meet *Dr. Gibson. Dr. Gibson*, this is my mother, *Mrs. Harrison.*

Person B: It's a pleasure to meet you, *Dr. Gibson.*

Person C: It's nice to meet you, too, *Mrs. Harrison.*

Can you think of another situation in which this type of problem might occur? For example, when might you call someone by his or her first name but then introduce him or her using a title and family name?

1. Discuss your example with the class.
2. Find two partners and practice your introductions using appropriate forms of address.

Sometimes it is difficult to know who gets introduced to whom when making introductions. There are no definite rules but you would be safe using these guidelines:

1. Introduce the person with whom you are most familiar to the other person.
2. If you are talking to someone and another person joins the conversation, introduce the newcomer to the person you are with.
3. Introduce a person to someone who is obviously older.

Consider the following pairs of people. Which person would you introduce to the other? Explain your answers.

1. Your teacher and a good friend.
2. Your husband or wife and your boss.
3. Your parent and a good friend.
4. Your grandmother and a classmate.
5. Your son and a coworker.

CONVERSATION PRACTICE WITH A FRIEND

1. Find two partners and practice these two conversations aloud.
2. Switch roles for extra practice.

Person A:	*Kathy,* I'd like you to meet *Professor Simon.*
Person B:	It's a pleasure to meet you, *Professor Simon.*
Person C:	It's nice to meet you, too, *Kathy.*

PEOPLE: Two students and a professor at a university.

INFORMATION TO CONSIDER: The two students are good friends. They are both women in their early twenties. The professor is a man in his late fifties. One of the students knows the professor; the other one has never met him before. Students generally use the title of Professor ______, Dr. ______, Mr. ______, Miss/Mrs./Ms. ______ when addressing a teacher. Teachers, however, generally call students by their first names.

INTRODUCTION: The two students see the professor between classes. The student who knows the professor introduces her friend to him.

Richard:	*Jim,* this is *Laura Martin. Laura,* this is *Jim Sutton.**
Jim:	Nice to meet you, *Laura.*
Laura:	Happy to meet you, too, *Jim.*

* You can also say: Jim Sutton, this is Laura Martin.

PEOPLE: Three people who work for the telephone company.

INFORMATION TO CONSIDER: Laura Martin is in her early thirties. The two men are in their forties. This is Laura's first day at the office. She has already met Richard but she doesn't know Jim. All three people have similar jobs and will work closely together in an informal setting. Richard wants to create a friendly, informal atmosphere with his introduction. He uses only the people's first and last names without titles.

INTRODUCTION: Richard and Laura have just come into the office where Jim is working. Richard introduces Laura to Jim.

Now You Try It

1. Read the following situations.

2. Find two partners and practice the introductions together.

3. You can choose the names of the people in each conversation. Think about which form of address is most appropriate for each person.

PEOPLE: Two cousins and an English teacher.

INFORMATION TO CONSIDER: Both cousins are women in their late teens. They have a very close relationship. One cousin is studying English in the U.S. The other cousin has come to the U.S. to visit her. The English teacher is a woman in her early twenties. The student and teacher have a friendly but formal relationship.

INTRODUCTION: The student has brought her cousin to class. She introduces her teacher to her cousin.

PEOPLE: Two friends and the mother of one of the friends.

INFORMATION TO CONSIDER: One of the friends is a woman; the other is a man. They are both in their twenties. Both people are students at a business college and have become close friends. The mother is in her early fifties. The young woman has never met the young man's mother.

INTRODUCTION: The two friends have gone to the man's house to study. The man introduces his friend to his mother.

PEOPLE: A married couple and a new neighbor.

INFORMATION TO CONSIDER: The husband and wife are middle-aged. The husband just met their new neighbor, who is a man in his late twenties. Both men are very relaxed and informal. They quickly form a friendship. The wife has never met the new neighbor.

INTRODUCTION: The husband, wife, and neighbor meet in the driveway. The husband introduces his wife to the neighbor.

PEOPLE: Three sales managers for different corporations.

INFORMATION TO CONSIDER: The three people are attending a big business conference. Two of the sales managers are women; the other is a man. All three people are middle-aged. One of the women and the man just met each other. Their relationship is strictly professional and quite formal. The man knows the other woman slightly. The two women don't know each other at all.

INTRODUCTION: The three people are talking. The man introduces the two women to each other.

PEOPLE: Three young men.

INFORMATION TO CONSIDER: All three men are in their late teens. One young man knows the other two very well, but those two people have never met each other. The three men are meeting in the park to play baseball together. All three are generally informal with people their own age.

INTRODUCTION: The two young men who don't know each other just arrived at the park. The other young man introduces them to each other.

PEOPLE: ______________________________

____

INFORMATION TO CONSIDER: ______________

____

____

____

INTRODUCTION: ______________________

____

____

What Would You Say?

Complete the following conversations. Explain why you chose the forms you did.

1. A college student is introducing a good friend to his new roommate. Create a possible conversation.

College student: ____________________

____

Friend: ____________________

____

Roommate: ____________________

____

How would this conversation change if the college student were introducing his good friend to a lawyer because his friend needed some legal advice? Create a possible conversation.

College student: ____________________

____

Friend: ____________________

____

Lawyer: ____________________

____

2. A wife is introducing her husband to the president of the company where she works. She doesn't know the president very well. Create a possible conversation.

Wife: ____________________

____

Husband: ____________________

____

President: ____________________

____

How would this conversation change if the wife were introducing her husband to one of her coworkers? She is very good friends with her coworker. Create a possible conversation.

Wife: ____________________

____

Husband: ____________________

____

Coworker: ____________________

____

3. You are a bank teller in a large bank. A new teller is beginning work today. How would you introduce the new teller to the vice-president in charge of loans? Create a possible conversation.

You: ____________________

____

New teller: ____________________

____

Vice-President: ____________________

____

How would this conversation change if you were introducing the new teller to one of the other tellers at the bank? You are very good friends with that person. Create a possible conversation.

You: ______________________________

____

New teller: ______________________________

____

Good friend: ______________________________

____

4. A young man is introducing his date to his father for the first time. Create a possible conversation.

Young man: ______________________________

____

Father: ______________________________

____

Date: ______________________________

____

How would this conversation change if the young man were introducing his date to his younger sister? Create a possible conversation.

Young man: ______________________________

____

Date: ______________________________

____

Sister: ______________________________

____

5. A young woman has convinced a good friend to join her exercise class. She is introducing her friend to another woman in the exercise class. Create a possible conversation.

Young woman: ______________________________

____

Good friend: ______________________________

____

Other woman: ______________________________

____

How would this conversation change if the young woman were introducing her good friend to the director of the physical-education program of a university? Create a possible conversation.

Young woman: ______________________________

____

Director: ______________________________

____

Good friend: ______________________________

____

Mix and Match

1. From the following list choose three pairs of people you might introduce to each other.
2. Write a brief description of the people. Include:
   Their ages;
   Their gender (if not already known);
   Your relationship with each person (Is it formal? Informal? Very close?);
   Their status (if important for the introduction).
3. Explain who gets introduced to whom.
4. Explain which form of address you use for each person.

people

Your mother or father
Your boss
Your teacher
Friends
Your lawyer
Your neighbors
Your father-in-law or mother-in-law
Your husband or wife
A coworker
Classmates
Your roommate

example:

People: My roommate and a coworker.

Description: My roommate is a woman in her twenties. We are very close. My coworker is a woman in her fifties. We have a friendly relationship but are not particularly close.

Introductions: I would introduce my roommate to my coworker because I'm more familiar with my roommate and because my coworker is older than my roommate.

Forms of address: I would introduce both women using their first and last names. I would not use any titles.

1. People: ____________________

   Description: ____________________

   ____

   Introductions: ____________________

   ____

   Forms of address: ____________________

   ____

2. People: ____________________

   Description: ____________________

   ____

Introductions: ______________________________

Forms of address: ______________________________

____

3. People: ______________________________

Description: ______________________________

____

Introductions: ______________________________

____

Forms of address: ______________________________

____

1. When you finish, discuss your choices with the group.
2. Find two partners and together choose one of your pairs of people around whom you can create an introduction.
3. Practice your introduction several times and then present it to the group.

Introducing Yourself

You can introduce yourself by saying:

I'd like to introduce myself.	↑ formal	
I don't think we've been introduced.		
I don't think we've met.		
Have we met before?		My name's *Liz Smith.* *
I don't think you know me.		
Hello.		
Hi.	↓ informal	

* You can also say: I'm *Liz Smith.*

Some replies:

How do you do?	↑ formal
(It's a) pleasure to meet you.	
(It's) nice to meet you.	
(I'm) glad to meet you.	
(I'm) happy to meet you.	
Hello.	
Hi.	↓ informal

FOR A BETTER UNDERSTANDING

When introducing themselves in English, people generally give their first and family names. For example:

Hello, my name's Terry Green.

However, in very informal situations, people sometimes just give their first names. For example:

Hi, my name's Terry.

Can you think of some informal situations in which you might introduce yourself using only your first name? Share your examples with the group. Can you think of some situations in which a person might formally introduce himself or herself using a title and family name? Share your examples with the group.

CONVERSATION PRACTICE WITH A FRIEND

1. Find a partner and practice these two conversations aloud.
2. Switch roles for extra practice.

Person A:	I don't think we've met. My name's *Bill Campbell*.
Person B:	I'm happy to meet you, *Bill*.
Person A:	It's nice to meet you, too.

Person A:	Hi, I'm *Bill Campbell*.
Person B:	Nice to meet you, *Bill*. I'm *Kelly Jones*.
Person A:	Nice to meet you, too.

PEOPLE: An academic advisor and a new student.

INFORMATION TO CONSIDER: The student is a twenty-year-old man. He is just starting classes at the English Language Center. The academic advisor is a middle-aged woman. They have never met each other before.

INTRODUCTION: The new student sees his academic advisor. He walks over to her and introduces himself.

PEOPLE: Two new students at the English Language Center.

INFORMATION TO CONSIDER: Both people are the same age. One student is a young man; the other is a young woman. They don't know each other but are sitting together with a group of friends. The situation is very informal.

INTRODUCTION: Bill realizes that he is sitting next to a student he doesn't know. He turns to her and introduces himself.

Now You Try It

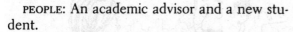

1. Read the following situations.
2. Find a partner and practice the introductions together.
3. You can choose the names of the people in each conversation. Think about which form of address is most appropriate for each person.

PEOPLE: A graduate student and a chairperson of the chemistry department.

INFORMATION TO CONSIDER: The graduate student is a man in his late twenties. The chairperson is a man in his early forties. They have never met.

INTRODUCTION: The graduate student made an appointment with the chairperson to learn about the chemistry department at this university. He walks into the chairperson's office and introduces himself.

PEOPLE: A pharmacy manager and an applicant for a job.

INFORMATION TO CONSIDER: The applicant for the job is a young woman in her late teens. The manager is a man in his late fifties.

INTRODUCTION: The young woman walks into the pharmacy. There is no receptionist. She goes to the manager and introduces herself. The young woman would really like to get the job at the pharmacy, so she tries to make a good impression on the manager.

PEOPLE: A receptionist in a dentist's office and a new patient.

INFORMATION TO CONSIDER: The receptionist is a young woman in her early twenties. The new patient is a middle-aged woman. This is her first appointment with this dentist.

INTRODUCTION: The new patient introduces herself to the receptionist and says she is here for her first dental appointment.

PEOPLE: A swim-team coach and a new team member.

INFORMATION TO CONSIDER: Both the coach and the team member are women in their early twenties. The coach is very friendly and casual. She likes swim-team practice to be very informal.

INTRODUCTION: This is the new team member's first swim practice. She walks up to the coach and introduces herself.

PEOPLE: Two salespeople in a large department store.

INFORMATION TO CONSIDER: Both salespeople are men. One man has worked in the department store for several years. He is in his forties. The other just started to work there today. He is twenty-one years old.

INTRODUCTION: The young man who just began working wants to get to know the other salesperson. He introduces himself.

PEOPLE: ______________________________

____

INFORMATION TO CONSIDER: ______________________________

____

____

INTRODUCTION: ______________________________

____

____

Rotation Role Play

This is John Drake and several people who know him. John Drake is sixty years old. He's married and is a professor of English at a university in an average-size city.

Name:	John Drake	Cynthia Peters	Kathy Drake
Relationship to John:		his student	his wife

Name:	Ree Douglas	Jamey Brown	Teresa Ross
Relationship to John:	his doctor	his minister	a colleague

In the following chart, write which form of address you think each person would use when talking to John. Also write which form of address you think John would use when talking to each of them. You can use:

1. A first name;
2. A title and a family name;
3. A term of endearment.*

*Some terms of endearment include: *Honey, Dear, Sweetie, Sugar, Angel, Pal, Buddy, Sweetheart.*

In some cases, more than one form of address is possible. Choose the one you think is best. Be prepared to discuss your answers.

Person	***What would that person call John?***	***What would John call that person?***
Cynthia Peters	________	________
Kathy Drake	________	________
Teresa Ross	________	________
Ree Douglas	________	________
Jamey Brown	________	________

Now complete the chart for Jennifer Pryer and her associates. Jennifer is a twenty-year-old student who has an internship in a big legal firm. She lives in the same city as John Drake.

Name:	Jennifer Pryer	George Wilson	Henry Hughes
Relationship to Jennifer:		her boyfriend	a lawyer in the firm

Name:	Maria Harper	Scott Fuller	Jack Park
Relationship to Jennifer:	her best friend	her landlord	a judge

Person	***What would that person call Jennifer?***	***What would Jennifer call that person?***
George Wilson	________	________
Henry Hughes	________	________
Maria Harper	________	________
Scott Fuller	________	________
Jack Park	________	________

situation

Today there is a town meeting where these twelve people live. All twelve people are at the meeting. Before the meeting begins, the people are introducing themselves to each other.

directions

1. Divide into groups of twelve people.
2. Become one of the twelve people at the meeting.
3. Make a name tag for yourself so that everyone can easily identify you.
4. Walk around and introduce yourself to some of the people you don't know. For example, John Drake's wife knows her husband, his doctor, and his minister; however, she probably doesn't know Jennifer Pryer or her boyfriend.
5. After introducing yourself to several people, find two people you'd like to introduce to each other.

One-Liners

1. Find a partner(s) and choose one of the conversation lines.
2. Together create a conversation around that line.
3. Present your role play to the group.

conversation 1

LINE: "Hi, I don't think we've met. My name's (your name). I just moved in next door."

PEOPLE: Two next-door neighbors.

SITUATION: One person just moved into the neighborhood. That person is introducing himself or herself to someone in the neighborhood.

conversation 2

LINE: "(name), I'd like you to meet my fiancé, (name). We're getting married next week."

PEOPLE: Two friends and a fiancé of one of the friends.

SITUATION: Two friends who haven't seen each other for a long time run into each other at a restaurant. One of the friends is with his or her fiancé. That person introduces the fiancé to the other friend.

conversation 3

LINE: "It's a pleasure to meet you, Ms. (name). You're the first newscaster I've ever met."

PEOPLE: A newscaster and a news-program viewer.

SITUATION: A person who watches news every night is visiting the news station. He or she gets to meet one of the newscasters at the station.

conversation 4

LINE: "Dr. (name), do you know my husband, (name)?"

PEOPLE: A married couple and a medical doctor.

SITUATION: A husband and wife are at a party. The wife, who is a nurse, sees one of the doctors with whom she works at the hospital. She introduces the doctor to her husband.

conversation 5

LINE: "Have we met before? My name's (your name)."

PEOPLE: Two strangers.

SITUATION: Two students are sitting in a student lounge between classes. One student introduces himself or herself to the other one.

conversation 6

LINE: "Hello, my name's (your name). I have an interview with Mrs. Andrews at three o'clock."

PEOPLE: A receptionist for a construction company and a person who has an interview.

SITUATION: The person who has an interview for a job introduces himself or herself to the receptionist.

Nonverbal Introductions

In addition to verbal expressions, people also use nonverbal body language when making introductions. When we make nonverbal introductions, we use our bodies instead of words to make the introductions. Everyone uses nonverbal body language when speaking. However, the specific manner in which it is used varies from culture to culture.

Here are some important features of nonverbal introductions for North Americans:

- Eye Contact
- Relative Distance Between Speakers
- Facial Expressions
- Handshaking
- Use of Hands and Head to Introduce People

Discussion Activity

Discuss these questions together. When answering these questions, consider how age, gender, and status might affect your responses.

1. How do North Americans look at each other when making introductions? Do they make direct eye contact? Do they glance around from person to person?
2. Compared to your culture, does it seem that North Americans stand close together or far apart in formal introductions? How about in informal introductions?
3. Generally speaking, what kind of facial expressions do North Americans have when making introductions? Are they reserved? Do they smile a lot?
4. How do North Americans shake hands when meeting other people? Do they always shake hands in introductions? In what situations are people most likely to shake hands?
5. How do North Americans use their hands and heads to introduce other people? Does this vary according to whether a person is in a formal or informal situation?
6. How is nonverbal body language used in introductions in your country? Would any of the uses of nonverbal body language mentioned here be considered silly or impolite in your country?

Role Plays

Following are five introduction situations. After you read each one, indicate whether the situation is formal or informal by circling the appropriate response.

Explain how you would use body language in each situation. Be sure to state how the people's age, gender, and status affected your decision.

situations

1. A man sees his favorite sports star at a snopping center. He walks up to the sports star and introduces himself.

   formal *informal*

   Appropriate nonverbal body language: ____________________

   ____

2. There is a party going on. A hostess is introducing a man and a woman. They are interested in getting to know each other better but are too shy to introduce themselves.

   formal *informal*

   Appropriate nonverbal body language: ____________________

   ____

3. Two young women are in their school cafeteria. They are both sitting by themselves. One woman walks over to the other woman and introduces herself.

   formal *informal*

   Appropriate nonverbal body language: ____________________

   ____

4. Three men are meeting each other at a nice restaurant for an important business lunch. Two of the men have never met each other. The third man is introducing them.

   formal *informal*

   Appropriate nonverbal body language: ____________________

   ____

5. A woman is going to a doctor for the first time. The nurse takes her into the doctor's office and introduces them to each other.

   formal *informal*

   Appropriate nonverbal body language: ____________________

   ____

directions

1. Find one or two partners (depending on the situation) with whom you can act out one of these situations. Pay special attention to the nonverbal body language.
2. Practice the conversation together. Use anything in the room as a prop.

3. When you know the conversation, present it to the class. Before you begin, give a brief explanation of your role play.
4. After you present your role play, have the others discuss how you used nonverbal body language in your introduction.

Look at the following photographs. Discuss how nonverbal body language is being used in each introduction. Do you think each introduction is formal or informal? Why?

Photograph taken by Jim Farley.

1. ____________________

Photograph taken by Teresa Farley.

2. ____________________

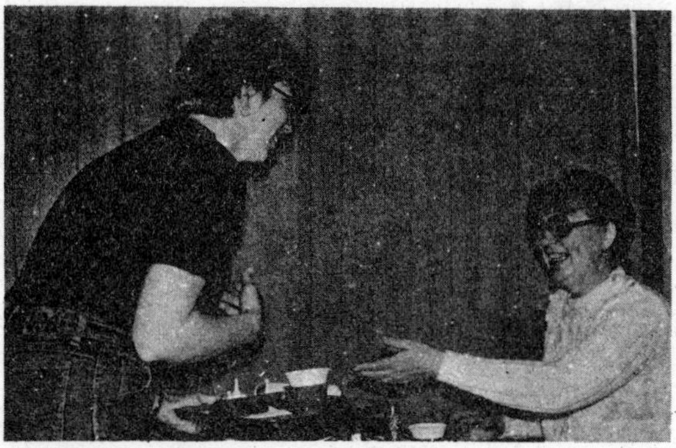
Photograph taken by Jim Farley.

3. ____________________

Photograph taken by Jim Farley.

4. ____________________

Making Small Talk After Introductions

What do people talk about after the introductions are made? In English there are certain "safe" topics which people frequently bring up when they first meet. These topics are often called *small talk.* Four common areas of small talk are:

1. A person's personal background;
2. A person's work/educational background;
3. A person's special interests (such as sports, music, politics);
4. The weather.

Following is a chart of small-talk topics. It includes one polite and one impolite question in each category. Questions considered impolite to ask right away are usually quite personal or put people on the defensive. These same questions may be perfectly acceptable to ask once you become better acquainted with the person; however, if asked too soon, such questions may make the other person angry or embarrassed.

directions

In each category of small talk there is a space for you to add one question you think is appropriate and one question you think is not. When you have completed the chart, go over it with the other people in the class. You might also want to briefly talk about how these areas of small talk differ from those in your country.

small-talk topics	*you might want to ask:*	*it's impolite to ask:*
A person's personal background	Where do you live? ________________	How much is your rent? ________________
A person's work or educational background	What kind of work do you do? ________________	How much money do you earn? ________________
A person's special interests	Are you interested in classical music? ________________	What religion are you? ________________
The weather	Are you enjoying all this snow we're having? ________________	Why is the weather in your city so terrible? ________________

Rotation Role Play

Once you have asked someone a question, you can usually continue the conversation by asking several related questions. By asking a few questions, you can often get past the first awkward minutes of meeting someone and have an interesting conversation.

Read the following question-and-response sequences. Think of three possible follow-up questions to each answer and write them in the spaces provided.

example

Question: *Where do you live?*
Answer: *I live in an apartment on 34th Street.*

1. Do you like your apartment?
2. Is it a convenient place to live?
3. Do you know any of your neighbors?

1. Question: *What do you do?*
   Answer: *I'm a pilot for United Airlines.*
   1. ____________________
   2. ____________________
   3. ____________________
2. Question: *Are you interested in sports?*
   Answer: *Yes, I really like football and hockey.*
   1. ____________________
   2. ____________________
   3. ____________________
3. Question: *Are you working or going to school?*
   Answer: *I'm a student at Boston University.*
   1. ____________________
   2. ____________________
   3. ____________________
4. Create your own conversation.
   Question: ____________________
   Answer: ____________________
   1. ____________________
   2. ____________________
   3. ____________________

role-play directions:

1. Imagine that everyone in the class is at a "beginning of the semester" party. You don't know each other.
2. Introduce yourself to someone at the party.
3. After the introductions are made, ask your partner one of the questions just listed: Where do you live? What do you do? Are you interested in sports?

4. Answer your partner's questions with actual information about yourself.
5. Ask an appropriate follow-up question. Remember that you'll both be asking each other several questions. In a conversation, there is no established order for asking questions. Alternate asking them in an order that seems comfortable to you.
6. Try to meet and speak with at least three people at the party.

The Interview

1. Find a partner; choose someone you don't know very well yet.
2. Introduce yourself to each other.
3. You have five minutes to find out everything you can about the other person using the areas of small talk listed on page 22. When your partner answers a question, try to ask one or several related questions.
4. You can make some notes to help you remember your partner's answers. When you've finished, share your information with the group.
5. If there is interest, you could repeat the activity. This time introduce yourself as a famous person about whom you know something. (Example: Sophia Loren, Napoleon Bonaparte, or Mao Tse Tung.)

COMMUNITY EXERCISES

Ask a friend to introduce you to an English-speaking acquaintance. Maybe your friend could introduce you to a relative, a coworker, a neighbor, and so on. Have a short conversation with that person using one or several of the areas of small talk to get you started.

directions:

Following is a chart to fill in *after* your conversation. Don't have the chart with you during the conversation; it might be very distracting. Plan to discuss your experience with your classmates. Good luck! You may make a new friend.

questions	*example*	*your answer*
Whom did you meet? Age? Gender? Status?	My friend's cousin.	
Which expression did your friend use to introduce you?	Margaret, this is Angela.	
What reply did you give?	Nice to meet you, Angela.	
What reply did the other person give?	Hi.	
How did the three of you use nonverbal body language during the introduction?	Smiling; direct eye contact.	
List one question you asked to make small talk.	Where are you from?	
List one follow-up question you asked.	Do you miss your family?	

Go to one of the following places in your community and find out what they do, what services they offer, how they work, and so on. Ask your teacher for some additional suggestions if none of these places interests you.

The local newspaper office;

The local YMCA or YMHA;

The local humane society;

The local chapter of the Better Business Bureau;

A local children's theater.

When you go, introduce yourself and ask several questions. Listen carefully to the people's answers and try to ask some follow-up questions.

directions:

When you have finished your conversation, complete the following chart. Plan to discuss your experience with the class.

questions	*your answer*
Where did you go?	
To whom did you talk? Age? Status? Gender?	
What reply did the other person give?	
How did you use nonverbal body language during the introduction?	
List one question you asked to obtain some information.	
List one follow-up question you asked.	
Did the other person ask you any questions? What was one?	

PUTTING IT TOGETHER

If you've learned this chapter well, you should be able to: (1) introduce yourself; (2) introduce other people; (3) carry on a brief conversation; and (4) know appropriate forms of address to use in a variety of situations. The following exercise gives you the opportunity to put these skills together.

role-play directions:

1. Following are several role-play situations. Find a partner(s) and together choose a role play that interests you.
2. Read the *Situation and Setting* sections carefully. Decide together which expressions, forms of address, and nonverbal body language are most appropriate for your roles.
3. Pay special attention to details and props. This makes your role play more realistic and fun. A list of details to consider is included in each role play.
4. Practice your conversation several times. When you feel comfortable with your conversation, present it to the class.
5. Before you begin, give some details of the players, their relationships to each other, and the situation and setting.

1. SITUATION AND SETTING: It is the first week of classes. Two people are sitting in the cafeteria at the end of the day. They don't know each other. One person introduces himself or herself to the other person. They have a brief conversation using some small-talk topics. A good friend of one of the people walks into the cafeteria. That person introduces the good friend to the other person. They also have a short conversation.

PLAYERS: There are three students. Two of the students are good friends. The third student doesn't know the other two.

DETAILS TO CONSIDER:

Your names	Cafeteria setting
Forms of address	Your topics of conversation
The name of your school	Nonverbal body language

2. SITUATION AND SETTING: Two workers in a large company are having a cup of coffee in the workers' lounge. They don't know each other although they've seen each other several times. One person introduces himself or herself to the other person. They have a brief conversation using some small-talk topics to get to know each other better.

PLAYERS: There are two coworkers in a large company. They don't know each other.

DETAILS TO CONSIDER:

Your names	Company lounge setting
Forms of address	Your topics of conversation
The name of your company	Nonverbal body language

3. SITUATION AND SETTING: A student is starting a new semester today. He or she walks into the classroom. The teacher is writing on the chalkboard. The student goes up to the teacher and introduces himself or herself. They have a brief conversation using some small-talk topics. (The teacher would probably begin the small talk.) One of the student's friends comes into the classroom. The student introduces the friend to the teacher and the three of them have a brief conversation.

PLAYERS: There is one teacher and two students who are good friends.

DETAILS TO CONSIDER:

Your names	Your topics of conversation
Forms of address	Nonverbal body language
Classroom setting with a chalkboard	

4. SITUATION AND SETTING: Two people have (separately) gone to a city park to enjoy the afternoon. Neither person has lived in this city very long. They are both sitting on the same park bench eating ice-cream cones. Suddenly they notice each other. One person introduces himself or herself to the other person. They have a brief conversation using some small-talk topics.

PLAYERS: There are two newcomers to a city. They are both men or both women. One person is much older than the other one.

DETAILS TO CONSIDER:

Your names	Park setting with a bench
Your backgrounds	(Imaginary) ice-cream cones
Forms of address	Nonverbal body language

Sticky Situations

Discuss these situations together.

1. You're talking to a friend and a person you don't know. Your friend forgot to introduce you to the other person. What can you do?
2. You just introduced yourself to someone. That person greeted you but forgot to tell you his or her name. What should you do?

CHAPTER 2

GREETINGS
GOODBYES

- Greetings
- Making Small Talk After Greetings
- Goodbyes
- Nonverbal Greetings and Goodbyes

Greetings

You can greet someone by saying:*

Good *morning* (*afternoon, evening*).	↑ formal	How are you?
Hello.		How are you doing?
Hi.		How are things?
	↓ informal	How's it going?

*If you haven't seen someone for a long time, you can follow your greeting with: It's been such a long time, or It's so good to see you again.

Some replies:

	Fine		↑ formal	
	(Very) good.	(thank you).		
	Great.			And you?
(I'm)	All right.			How are you?
	OK.			How about you?
	Not too bad.			What about you?
		(thanks).	↓ informal	

FOR A BETTER UNDERSTANDING

Some greetings seem to ask how a person actually feels at the moment. For example:

How are you?
or
How are you doing?

These greetings, however, are just different ways of saying, "Hello." Their message is impersonal. For this reason, replies to such greetings are usually *positive* in meaning even if the person doesn't feel good at that moment. A person only gives an honest *negative* reply to a very close friend or family member. Two negative replies are:

I feel horrible.
or
I'm really sick.

CONVERSATION PRACTICE WITH A FRIEND

1. Find a partner and practice these two conversations aloud.
2. Switch roles for extra practice.

Person A: Good afternoon, Dr. Martin.
Person B: Hello, Chris. How are you today?
Person A: I'm fine, thank you. How are you?
Person B: Fine, thank you.

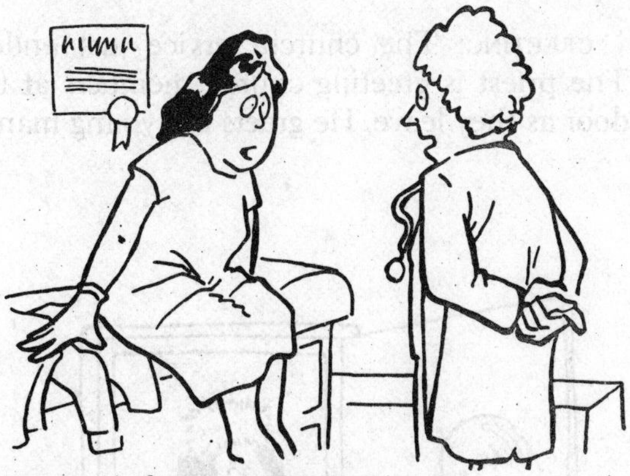

PEOPLE: A doctor and her patient.

INFORMATION TO CONSIDER: The doctor is a middle-aged woman. The patient is a young woman in her twenties. The woman has been a patient of the doctor for a few years. Their relationship is strictly professional.

GREETING: The patient has come for her yearly checkup with the doctor. She walks into the doctor's office and greets her.

Person A: Hi Amy. How's it going?
Person B: Great! How about you?
Person A: Not too bad.

PEOPLE: Two friends.

INFORMATION TO CONSIDER: Both people are young women in their late teens. They have been close friends since childhood.

GREETING: The two friends run into each other at the neighborhood laundromat.

Now You Try It

1. Read the following situations.
2. Find a partner and practice the greetings together.
3. You can choose the names of the people in each conversation. Think about which form of address is most appropriate for each person.

PEOPLE: Two friends.

INFORMATION TO CONSIDER: Both people are middle-aged. One person is a man; the other is a woman. They used to live next door to each other, but the man moved to another part of the city. While they were neighbors, they had a friendly relationship; however, they haven't seen each other since the man moved.

GREETING: The two friends run into each other at a movie. They greet each other.

PEOPLE: A priest and a church member.

INFORMATION TO CONSIDER: The church member is a man in his early twenties. He just joined this church and doesn't know the priest very well yet.

GREETING: The church service just ended. The priest is greeting church members at the door as they leave. He greets the young man.

PEOPLE: A husband and a wife.

INFORMATION TO CONSIDER: Both people are in their early fifties. They have been happily married for several years.

GREETING: The wife just got home from a hard day at work. The husband is already home. He greets her when she walks in the door.

PEOPLE: A professor and a student.

INFORMATION TO CONSIDER: The professor is a man in his early thirties. The student is a twenty-year-old man who took a course from the professor three semesters ago. The two people had a friendly relationship during the course, but they don't know each other very well.

GREETING: The student is going to take another course with the professor. He greets his professor when he walks into the classroom on the first day.

PEOPLE: An immigration officer and a visiting foreign student.

INFORMATION TO CONSIDER: The immigration officer is a middle-aged woman. The student is an eighteen-year-old woman. She is having some problems with her visa and must talk to the immigration officer. The officer and student have talked together a few times. Their conversations are always very businesslike.

GREETING: The student sits down at the immigration officer's desk and greets her.

PEOPLE: ______________________________

____

INFORMATION TO CONSIDER: ______________________________

____

____

____

GREETING: ______________________________

____

____

What Would You Say?

1. You are at a party and notice a person you used to work with several years ago. You walk over to him or her and say:

   ____

2. You are locking the front door of your apartment as you leave for work. You notice that your next-door neighbor is also locking his front door. You turn to your neighbor and say:

   ____

3. It's Monday morning. Your boss just came in your office and greeted you. You reply:

____

4. You are at the airport waiting for your sister to arrive. You haven't seen her in a year. When she gets off the plane, you run up to her and say:

____

5. You are shopping in a furniture store. One of the salespeople comes up and greets you. You reply:

____

6. You are a receptionist in an optometrist's* office. One of your regular patients has come for an appointment. When she walks in, you say:

____

7. Your grandmother has just called you long distance on the telephone. You haven't talked to each other in several months. She has just greeted you. You reply by saying:

____

8. You and a coworker are passing each other in the office hallway. It's the first time you've seen each other that day. You greet your coworker by saying:

____

9. You are checking books out of the library. When you walk up to the checkout desk, the librarian greets you. You reply:

____

10. It is the beginning of the fall semester at your school. At registration you notice a classmate you haven't seen all summer. You wave to him and say:

____

* An *optometrist* is a doctor who treats people with eye problems.

Rotation Role Play

List pairs of people who might greet each other.

1. Two coworkers
2. ____
3. ____
4. ____
5. ____
6. ____

Imagine that you feel:	
• Surprised	• Relieved
• Extremely happy	• Excited
• Nervous	• Shy
• Uninterested	• Shocked

directions:

1. Find a partner. Together choose a pair of people from your list.
2. Greet each other using one of the emotions just listed.
3. Repeat steps two and three several times.

Making Small Talk After Greetings

When you greet someone, it's nice to be able to say a little more than just "Hello." When greeting people, North Americans often use the small-talk topics discussed in Chapter One in order to get a conversation going. These topic areas are:

1. A person's personal background;
2. A person's work/educational background;
3. A person's special interests (such as sports, music, politics);
4. The weather.

Because you already know the person you are greeting, the kinds of questions you ask when making small talk are different from those you ask when meeting someone for the first time.

directions:

Following is a chart of small-talk topics. There is a space in each category for you to add a question or statement you think might be appropriate. Discuss your choices together. Do any of the questions or statements seem inappropriate? You might also want to talk about how these areas of small talk differ from those in your country.

small-talk topics	*example*	*you could also say*
A person's personal background	How is your wife?	____________
A person's work or educational background	How is your job going?	____________
A person's special interests	There's going to be a big jazz festival this weekend. Are you going?	____________
The weather	Have you ever seen such a beautiful day?	____________

Rotation Role Play

Once you have asked someone a question, you can continue the conversation by asking several related questions.

Read the following question-and-response sequences. Think of three possible follow-up questions to each answer and write them in the spaces provided.

example

Question: *How is your wife?*
Answer: *Great! She just got a new job.*

1. Where does she work?
2. What does she do exactly?
3. Does she like it?

1. Question: *How is your job going?*
   Answer: *Not so good. I had to work late every day this week.*
   1. ______
   2. ______
   3. ______
2. Question: *Are you still jogging for exercise?*
   Answer: *Yes, I jog two miles every morning.*
   1. ______
   2. ______
   3. ______
3. Question: *Have you ever seen such a beautiful day?*
   Answer: *No, I'm going to go bike riding so I can enjoy it.*
   1. ______
   2. ______
   3. ______
4. Create your own conversation.
   Question: ______
   Answer: ______
   1. ______
   2. ______
   3. ______

role-play directions:

1. Imagine that it is the first morning of class after a weekend or a week's vacation.
2. Greet someone and then have a brief conversation using the four areas of small-talk presented on page 35.

3. Ask questions that are specifically relevant for the person to whom you are talking. For example, if someone in the class likes to go to the movies every Friday night, you might ask that person which movie he or she saw.
4. Answer your partner with actual information about yourself.
5. After your partner has answered your question, ask an appropriate follow-up question. Remember that you'll both be asking each other questions. Alternate asking them in an order that seems comfortable to you.
6. Try to speak with at least three different people in your class.

Choose the Dialogue

1. Following are two conversations. Find a partner to help you practice them. Before you begin, cover up your partner's side of the dialogue.
2. Person A begins the conversation by reading 1. Person B chooses one of the replies in 2 and reads it to Person A.
3. Person A then reads the appropriate answer in 3. (There will be only one correct response.)
4. Continue the conversation. It's very important to listen to what your partner says.

person a	*person b*
1. Hi (partner's name). How's it going?	*2.* Fine. How about you? or Oh, not so good.
3. Really? What's wrong? or Not bad, thanks. How is your daughter? Is she still sick?	*4.* Yes, she still has a fever and a bad cough. or My checkbook was stolen yesterday.
5. Does your doctor know what the problem is? or Where was it stolen?	*6.* On the bus. I wasn't paying attention. or Well, he thinks it's a new kind of virus.
7. How long does this type of virus last? or Did you call the police?	*8.* Yes, but they said they couldn't do much to help me. or No more than ten days. So, she'll probably feel better by this weekend.

Goodbyes

Here are some ways to bring a conversation to a close:

	Thank you for your time.	formal ↑
	I really must go.	
	I'll let you go.	
(It's late) *	I should be going.	
	I'd better go now.	
	I have to run.	
	I've got to go now.	↓ informal

* You can also say: I didn't realize it was so late, or Look at the time.

Here are some goodbyes which might follow:

Good night.	formal ↑
Goodbye.	
Bye.	
Bye-bye.	
See you *later* (soon, tomorrow . . .).	
Take care.	
So long.	
Take it easy.	↓ informal

When North Americans are leaving each other permanently or for a long time, they use a different set of closings from those just listed.

Here are some long-term closings:

(It was) nice being here.	formal ↑
(It was) nice seeing you.	
(It was) good talking to you.	
Take care (of yourself).	
Keep in touch.	
Call/Write to me.	
I'll miss you.	↓ informal

Here are some goodbyes which might follow:

Goodbye.	formal ↑
Bye.	
Bye-bye.	
Take care.	
Take it easy.	↓ informal

FOR A BETTER UNDERSTANDING

When North Americans want to end a conversation, they often begin with some kind of conversation closing followed by a goodbye. Sometimes the goodbye can seem quite long. This is so the other person doesn't feel suddenly cut off. For this reason, it would not be unusual to hear a goodbye like this:

Person A: Oh, look at the time! I have to go now
Person B: OK. Bye-bye.
Person A: Take it easy. I'll see you later.

Sometimes it is difficult for a foreign student to know when to say goodbye in English. North Americans have several nonverbal cues that might suggest they wish the conversation to come to a close. Watch for them. Take turns demonstrating these cues in front of the class.

1. A person is looking at his or her watch a lot.
2. A person starts to stand up if sitting.
3. A person starts walking towards (or looking at) the door if standing.
4. A person is shuffling back and forth or fidgeting in a nervous manner.
5. A person is looking around the room at other people or things.

CONVERSATION PRACTICE WITH A FRIEND

1. Find a partner and practice these conversations aloud.
2. Switch roles for extra practice.

Person A: It was nice seeing you again, Dr. Stafford.
Person B: It was nice seeing you, too, Dr. Williams. Goodbye.
Person A: Goodbye.

PEOPLE: Two medical doctors.

INFORMATION TO CONSIDER: Both doctors are middle-aged. One is a man; the other is a woman. The two people don't know each other very well; their relationship is professional. In fact, they only see each other once a year at a state-wide medical convention.

GOODBYE: The medical convention just ended. The two doctors are in the lobby of the convention center getting ready to leave. They probably won't see each other for another year.

Person A: I'll miss you. Keep in touch.
Person B: OK. I'll write soon. Take care of yourself.
Person A: Bye-bye.
Person B: Bye.

PEOPLE: Two roommates at college.

INFORMATION TO CONSIDER: The roommates are both women in their early twenties. They are very close friends.

GOODBYE: It is the end of the school year. Both roommates are getting ready to go home for the summer. They won't see each other again until September.

Now You Try It

1. Read the following situations.
2. Find a partner and practice the goodbyes together.
3. You can choose the names of the people in each conversation. Think about which form of address is most appropriate.

PEOPLE: Two friends.

INFORMATION TO CONSIDER: Both friends are men in their early thirties. They have a close, friendly relationship and often socialize together.

GOODBYE: The two men run into each other while downtown shopping. They talk for a while. One man realizes that he is very late for an appointment at the barbershop and finishes the conversation.

PEOPLE: A father and a son.

INFORMATION TO CONSIDER: The son is twenty-one years old. He is getting ready for his third year in college. The father and son have a very close, loving relationship.

GOODBYE: The son is going to spend his third year in Mexico studying Spanish. He won't see his father for one year. They are at the airport saying goodbye.

PEOPLE: Two classmates.

INFORMATION TO CONSIDER: Both classmates are in their late twenties. One is a man; the other is a woman. They have a friendly relationship but are not very close. They only get together to study for exams.

GOODBYE: Both classmates are studying together at the library for a big exam. One student is very tired and wants to go home. He or she ends their conversation.

PEOPLE: Two businesspeople.

INFORMATION TO CONSIDER: Both people are middle-aged women. One woman is the president of an advertising agency. The other woman is an important client. The two people do not get together very often. When they do, it is to discuss business. Their relationship is strictly professional.

GOODBYE: The two women have just finished an important meeting. The client is getting ready to leave. They probably won't have another meeting for several months.

PEOPLE: A bartender and a customer.

INFORMATION TO CONSIDER: The bartender is a man in his late twenties. The customer is a man in his late fifties. The customer comes to this bar frequently. The bartender and customer have known each other for several years. They have a friendly but not particularly close relationship.

GOODBYE: The bartender and customer have been talking off and on all evening. The customer is getting ready to leave and ends the conversation.

PEOPLE: ______________________

____

INFORMATION TO CONSIDER: ______________________

____

____

GOODBYE: ______________________

____

____

Multiple Choice

Read the following ten statements. Circle the goodbye which is *most appropriate* to the situation.

1. You are having an interview with an employer. A signal that he or she might want to end the conversation is:
   A. I'll miss you.
   B. Thank you for your time.
   C. It was nice being here.

2. You are having a special tutoring session with your professor. He or she says, "OK, let's call it a night." Your best reply is:
   A. See you tomorrow, Professor Martin.
   B. Keep in touch, Professor Martin.
   C. It was good talking to you again, Professor Martin

3. You are at the airport with your boyfriend or girlfriend. He or she is leaving on a two-month trip. An appropriate goodbye is:
   A. Write me. I'll miss you.
   B. It was nice being here.
   C. Bye. See you later.

4. You are talking with a good friend in the cafeteria. You notice it's time for you to go to class. An appropriate goodbye is:
   A. Thank you for your time.
   B. Write me. Good-bye.
   C. I'd better go now. Take it easy.

5. You are talking to one of your neighbors in your front yard on a Sunday morning. He or she says, "I'd better go now." An appropriate reply is:
   A. It was good seeing you again.
   B. Good night.
   C. Bye-bye. Take care.

6. You are getting off a plane. An appropriate goodbye to the flight attendant is:
   A. Keep in touch.
   B. Goodbye. Thank you.
   C. I'll miss you.

7. It's the end of a date with a friend. You frequently go out together. An appropriate goodbye is:
   A. It's been good talking to you again.
   B. Write me. Bye.
   C. Good night. See you tomorrow.

8. You just made a complaint to your landlord because you have no hot water in your apartment. To politely end the conversation, you should say:
   A. Look at the time! I've got to go.
   B. Thank you, Mr. Baker, I'll let you go now. Goodbye.
   C. Keep in touch.

9. You just had a checkup at your dentist's office. An appropriate good bye is:
   A. It was nice seeing you, Dr. Black. Goodbye.
   B. So long, Joe.
   C. Call me, Dr. Black.

10. You are having a conversation with your boss. You say, "It's late. I'll let you go now." The best reply she could give is:
   A. OK. Bye-bye.
   B. It was nice being here. Goodbye.
   C. Keep in touch. Bye.

One-Sided Dialogue

1. Read the following dialogue. Only Person A's lines are given.
2. Fill in the dialogue for Person B. Read Person A's lines carefully. They give you hints about what Person B is saying.
3. When you complete the dialogue, practice it with someone.

This is a conversation between two friends. Person B has just started working as a high-school coach.

A: Hi (partner's name). How are you doing?

B: ______________________________

____

A: I'm fine, too. Tell me about your new job. Do you like it?

B: ______________________________

____

A: That's great! But I didn't know you were teaching football, swimming, *and* tennis. Are you going to go out of town for competitions?

B: ______________________________

____

A: Two weekends a month! You are going to be very busy this year.

B: ______________________________

______________________________?

A: Oh, my job is fine. I'm learning how to use a computer now. That's a lot of fun.

B: ______________________________

______________________________?

A: No, computers are really easy to use once you understand the basic principles.

B: ______________________________

____

A: You're right. It is late. I have to go to work, too.

B: ______________________________

A: Bye-bye.

Nonverbal Greetings and Goodbyes

In addition to verbal expressions, North Americans also use nonverbal body language when greeting people and saying goodbye. When we communicate nonverbal greetings and goodbyes, we use our bodies instead of words to say "Hello" and "Goodbye." Everyone uses nonverbal body language when speaking. However, the specific manner in which it is used varies from culture to culture.

Here are some important features of nonverbal greetings and goodbyes for North Americans:

- Eye Contact
- Relative Distance Between Speakers
- Facial Expression
- Handshaking
- Touching
- Hugging
- Kissing

Discussion Activity

Discuss these questions together. When answering these questions, consider how the age, gender, status, and relationship of the people affect your responses.

1. How do North Americans look at each other when making greetings or saying goodbye? Do they make direct eye contact? Do they glance around a lot?
2. Compared to your culture, does it seem that North Americans stand close together or far apart when formally greeting each other or saying goodbye? How about in informal greetings and goodbyes?
3. Generally speaking, what kind of facial expressions do North Americans have when greeting someone or saying goodbye? Are they reserved? Do they smile a lot?
4. How do North Americans shake hands when meeting someone? Do they always shake hands when greeting someone or saying goodbye? In what situations are people most likely to shake hands?
5. How is nonverbal body language used in greetings and goodbyes in your country? Would any of the uses of nonverbal body language mentioned previously be considered impolite or silly in your country?
6. Have two people volunteer to act out the following situations. Only use nonverbal body language; do not speak.

SITUATION ONE: You are both at the airport. You are two business executives. One person is the president of a large company; the other person is an important client of the company. Your relationship is very businesslike. The president of the company has come to the airport to meet the client. How would you greet each other?

SITUATION TWO: You are both at the airport. You are two close family members who haven't seen each other for several months. One family member has come to the airport to meet the other one. How would you greet each other?

As a group, discuss which nonverbal body language was used in each greeting. How were the greetings the same? How were they different? Now, act out these two situations again. This time imagine that the people are saying goodbye to each other.

Role Plays

Following are five situations in which people are greeting each other or saying goodbye. After you read each one, indicate whether the situation is formal or informal by circling the appropriate response.

Explain how you would use body language in each situation. Be sure to state how the age, gender, status, and relationship of the people in the role play affected your decisions.

situations:

1. A student is saying goodbye to his or her English teacher. The student has been accepted into an American university in another state.

   formal *informal*

   Appropriate nonverbal body language: ______________________________

   ____

2. Two coworkers who know each other well are greeting each other on Monday morning.

   formal *informal*

   Appropriate nonverbal body language: ______________________________

   ____

3. Two close friends are saying goodbye to each other. They'll see each other later tonight.

   formal *informal*

   Appropriate nonverbal body language: ______________________________

   ____

4. A parent and a child are saying goodbye to each other. The child, eighteen years old, is going away to college for the first time.

   formal *informal*

   Appropriate nonverbal body language: ______________________________

   ____

5. A visiting foreign student just finished a meeting with an immigration officer at the Immigration Office. They are saying goodbye to each other.

   formal *informal*

   Appropriate nonverbal body language: ______________________________

   ____

directions:

1. Find a partner with whom you can act out one of these situations. Pay special attention to the nonverbal body language.
2. Practice the conversation together. Use anything in the room as a prop.
3. When you know the conversation, present it to the class. Before you begin, give a brief explanation of your role play.
4. After you present your role play, have the others discuss how you used nonverbal body language in your greeting or goodbye.

Look at the following photographs. Discuss how nonverbal body language is being used in each greeting or goodbye. Do you think each interaction is formal or informal? Why?

Photograph taken by Teresa Farley.

Photograph taken by Haissam Chehab.

1. ______________________________

2. ______________________________

Photograph taken by Jim Farley.

Photograph taken by Teresa Farley.

3. ______________________________

4. ______________________________

COMMUNITY EXERCISES

Greet three people you know. Try to choose different types of people in both formal and informal situations. Fill in the following information:

Whom did you greet?	1. ____________	2. ____________	3. ____________
Which greetings and nonverbal body language did you use?	1. ____________ ____________ ____________	2. ____________ ____________ ____________	3. ____________ ____________ ____________
Which greetings and nonverbal body language did the other person use?	1. ____________ ____________ ____________	2. ____________ ____________ ____________	3. ____________ ____________ ____________

Make note of three people to whom you say goodbye. Try to consider different types of people in both formal and informal situations. Fill in the following information:

To whom did you say goodbye?	1. ____________	2. ____________	3. ____________
Which expressions and nonverbal body language did you use?	1. ____________ ____________ ____________	2. ____________ ____________ ____________	3. ____________ ____________ ____________
Which expressions and nonverbal body language did the other person use?	1. ____________ ____________ ____________	2. ____________ ____________ ____________	3. ____________ ____________ ____________

Listen to four pairs of people greeting or saying goodbye to each other. Try to find people in different kinds of situations. Listen to their greetings and goodbyes and then complete the chart on the following page.

	example	one	two	three	four
Who greeted or said goodbye to each other? (Just list types of people.)	Two school friends Both were men They greeted each other				
Which greetings or goodbyes did they use?	Hi. How are you doing? Not bad. How about you?				
Did they use any nonverbal body language?	Handshaking Smiling				
Did you hear any new greetings or goodbyes? Did you see any new nonverbal body language? Write them down if you can.	The two men patted each other on the back a lot.				

PUTTING IT TOGETHER

If you learned this chapter well, you should be able to: (1) greet someone you know; (2) carry on a brief conversation; and (3) close the conversation and say goodbye in a variety of situations. The following activities give you the opportunity to put these skills together and to review the information from Chapter One.

What Would You Say?

1. You are walking down the street and you see your mathematics teacher come out of a drugstore. You wave to her and say·

   ____

2. You are at a party with two friends. They don't know each other. You turn to them and say:

   ____

3. Your roommate has just introduced you to your new next-door neighbor, an elderly woman. You say to your new neighbor:

   ____

4. You have a checkup with your dentist this afternoon. You walk into your dentist's office and say:

   ____

5. You are having a conversation with a good friend. When you ask how he is, your friend replies that he was in a car accident last night. A good follow-up question might be:

   ____

6. Two of your parents' close friends asked you to spend the weekend in their home. Now you are getting ready to leave. You probably won't see them for a long time. Before you go, you say:

   ____

7. You just finished an important meeting with your academic advisor. To let you know the meeting has ended, your academic advisor says to you:

   ____

8. You've just met a new coworker for the first time at lunch. To get to know him or her better, you might ask:

   ____

Build-Up Role Plays

Create your own role play as a class (or in small groups if the class is large) using the following directions. Repeat the "Build-Up" process to create other role plays.

FIRST PERSON: Choose the functions which you want to use in the role play. Select them from this list:

Introducing Others	Small Talk
Introducing Yourself	Goodbyes/Conversation Closings
Greetings	

SECOND PERSON: Give a setting for the role play.

THIRD PERSON: Create a role play situation in that setting, including the players.

FOURTH PERSON: Name the important details to consider to make the role play realistic, including information about the players.

FIFTH, SIXTH, SEVENTH . . . PERSON: You are the players who act out the role play.

Sticky Situations

Discuss these situations together.

1. An acquaintance just gave you a friendly greeting but called you by someone else's name. What should you do?
2. You've tried to bring the conversation to a close a couple of times, but the other person just won't quit talking. How can you politely end the conversation?

CHAPTER 3

INVITATIONS

- Making and Accepting Invitations
- Refusing Invitations
- Avoiding Invitations

Making and Accepting Invitations

You can invite someone by saying:

	come to our house for dinner?
Would you like to . . .* (formal/informal)	go to the theater with me?
Do you want to . . . (informal)	go out to dinner?
	go to a movie with me?
or	
	getting a cup of coffee?
How about . . . (informal)	going shopping?
	going to the library with me?

*The phrase "Would you like to . . ." is pronounced differently depending on whether you use it to make a formal or an informal invitation. Carefully go over the pronunciation of this phrase with your teacher.

You can accept an invitation by saying:

	I'd be delighted.	formal	Thank you (very much) for asking.
	I'd like that very much.		
	That would be very nice.		
(Yes)	I'd love to.		
	Sure, that sounds like fun.		Thanks (a lot) for asking.
	Sure, that sounds great.	informal	

FOR A BETTER UNDERSTANDING

In English, people generally do not immediately make an invitation at the beginning of their conversation. When first greeting someone, they usually use some of the small-talk topics to lead into a conversation. After talking a while, they then appropriately make the invitation. Even if you know the other person well, it is considered polite to talk a few minutes before making an invitation. Making an invitation too quickly might seem forward or pushy.

1. Together think of an invitation one friend might make to another and write it on the chalkboard.

2. Have two people volunteer to act out the following scene:

You are two good friends who accidently meet while shopping downtown. Have a brief conversation using small-talk topics. When you think it's appropriate, one friend can make the invitation on the chalkboard to the other friend.

CONVERSATION PRACTICE WITH A FRIEND

1. Find a partner and practice these two conversations aloud.
2. Switch roles for extra practice.

Person A:	Would you like to go out to lunch tomorrow afternoon?
Person B:	Yes, I'd like that very much. Thank you for asking.

Person A:	Do you want to go to the football game tomorrow night?
Person B:	Yes,* sure, that sounds like fun. Thanks for asking.

PEOPLE: The president of a big company and an important client.

INFORMATION TO CONSIDER: The two people are in their late fifties. The president is a man; the important client is a woman. They don't know each other very well. Their relationship is strictly professional.

INVITATION: The president of the company is going to invite the client to lunch.

PEOPLE: Two good friends who go to the same school.

INFORMATION TO CONSIDER: Both students are twenty-one-year-old men. They have gone to school together for three years. They have a close, friendly relationship.

INVITATION: One friend is inviting the other to go to the football game tomorrow night.

*Before "Sure, that sounds like fun," or "Sure, that sounds great," *Yes* is pronounced *Yeah*. For example:
A: Would you like to go dancing?
B: Yeah, sure, that sounds great.

PEOPLE: A husband and a wife.

INFORMATION TO CONSIDER: The husband and wife have a very close, loving relationship. They are both in their early thirties.

INVITATION: The wife is inviting the husband to take a trip somewhere for the weekend. (You can decide the location of the trip.)

PEOPLE: A student and his English teacher.

INFORMATION TO CONSIDER: Both the teacher and the student are men. The teacher is middle-aged. The student is twenty years old. It is near the end of the semester. The teacher and the student have a friendly but professional relationship.

INVITATION: The student is inviting the teacher to a class party he is giving Friday night.

PEOPLE: Two medical assistants who work together in a hospital.

INFORMATION TO CONSIDER: Both medical assistants are men in their twenties. They see each other often in the hospital but rarely talk to each other. Their relationship at this point is very distant.

INVITATION: Both men just finished working for the day. One man invites the other to have a cup of coffee in the hospital cafeteria.

PEOPLE: Two teammates on a hockey team.

INFORMATION TO CONSIDER: Both students are twenty-year-old women. They are very good friends and have gone to school together for two years.

INVITATION: One friend is inviting the other to go camping this weekend.

PEOPLE: An accountant and her boss.

INFORMATION TO CONSIDER: The accountant is a person in her thirties who just started working in the accounting firm. The boss is a man in his early sixties. Their status is not the same. Their relationship is friendly but professional.

INVITATION: The accountant is inviting her boss and his wife to a quiet dinner party at her home.

PEOPLE: ______________________

INFORMATION TO CONSIDER: ______________________

INVITATION: ______________________

Rotation Role Play

List pairs of people who might invite each other to do something.

example

A boyfriend and a girlfriend

1. ______________________
2. ______________________
3. ______________________
4. ______________________
5. ______________________
6. ______________________

The person making the invitation must use one of the following verbs in his or her invitation:

- Watch
- Come
- Go
- Take a ride
- Get
- Run/jog
- Visit
- See
- Dance
- Play

Imagine that the other person accepts the invitation, feeling one of the following emotions:

- Astonished
- Happy
- Surprised
- Excited
- Nervous
- Frightened
- Wary
- Uninterested

directions:

1. Find a partner. Together choose a pair of people from your list.
2. Have one person make an appropriate invitation using one of the verbs just listed.
3. Have the other person accept the invitation using one of the emotions just listed.
4. Repeat steps one thru three several times.

What Would You Say?

1. Jerry has just bought two great tickets to a rock concert for tonight. He walks up to his girlfriend and says:
   ____
2. Sarah is really bored. She wants to do something exciting this weekend. When her roommate walks in the door, Sarah says:
   ____
3. Jim wants to ask his boss for a raise. He thinks it would be a good idea to take his boss out for a drink first. When Jim walks into his boss' office, he says:
   ____
4. This is your first day of work. A coworker just asked you to have a cup of coffee with her. You reply:
   ____
5. You just won a free trip for two to Rome. You call up your best friend on the phone and say:
   ____
6. You are very interested in modern American artists; your teacher is too. He just invited you to go with him to a special exhibit at the Museum of Fine Arts. You say:
   ____
7. Your brother just invited you to spend the weekend skiing in Colorado. You say:
   ____
8. You are very interested in an attractive person who works in your office. Now that you finally have the courage to ask her or him out, you walk up to her or his desk and say:

Refusing Invitations

There are times when someone invites you to do something and you'd like to say "No." There are many ways to politely turn down an invitation. In addition to refusing the invitation, in English you also need to give some kind of explanation. (I have to study for an exam. My son's having his birthday party tonight . . .)

Following are some expressions used to turn down invitations. Suggested explanations for refusing invitations are discussed in more detail in the next section.

AN INVITATION: Would you like to go to dinner with me tonight?

You can refuse an invitation by saying:

Thank you for asking but . . .	I'm afraid I can't.	formal ↑	
	I'm sorry I can't.		
	I have other plans.		(and your explanation)
	Maybe some other time.		
Thanks for asking but . . . *	I'm already busy.		
	I have too much to do.	↓ informal	

* You can also say: I'd like to but . . . , I'd love to but . . . , or I wish I could but . . . .

FOR A BETTER UNDERSTANDING

When North Americans refuse an invitation, they usually give some kind of explanation when they are turning it down. For example:

Person A: Would you like to go to the new Chinese exhibit at the museum?
Person B: Thank you for asking, but I'm afraid I can't. I have to go to the airport to pick up my sister. She's going to visit me for a week.

This might seem like a very long way to say "No" to someone. In English, however, it is considered impolite or a little abrupt to just say, for example:

Thanks, but I have other plans.
or
I'm just too tired.

Such abruptness could easily indicate to the other person that you don't ever want to do anything with him or her. For this reason, it's important to learn how to politely refuse an invitation in English. Sometimes when you refuse an invitation, you can immediately make another invitation to let the person know that you are genuinely interested in getting together.

CONVERSATION PRACTICE WITH A FRIEND

1. Find a partner and practice these two conversations aloud.
2. Switch roles for extra practice.

Person A:	Would you like to go to a jazz concert with me tomorrow night?
Person B:	Thank you for asking, but I'm afraid I can't. I have a swimming lesson tomorrow night. How about going to a concert some other time?
Person A:	Yes, I'd love to. Thank you for asking.

Person A:	Do you want to go to the beach with me this weekend?
Person B:	I'm sorry, but I can't. I have to write a paper for my economics course. How about going to the baseball game Monday night when you get back?
Person A:	Sure, that sounds great.

PEOPLE: A man and a woman who just met in a health club.

INFORMATION TO CONSIDER: The man and the woman are both in their late thirties. The man is a professor of music. The woman is the business manager of a bookstore. They don't know each other very well yet.

FIRST INVITATION: The man invites the woman to go to a jazz concert tomorrow night.

SECOND INVITATION: The woman invites the man to go to a concert next Friday night.

PEOPLE: Two roommates.

INFORMATION TO CONSIDER: Both students are twenty-five-year-old men. They have been roommates for two years and have a close, friendly relationship.

FIRST INVITATION: One roommate invites the other to go to the beach for the weekend.

SECOND INVITATION: The other roommate invites the first to go to the baseball game Monday night.

Now You Try It

1. Read the following situations.
2. Find a partner and practice the invitations using the preceding conversations as models.

PEOPLE: Two sisters still living at home.

INFORMATION TO CONSIDER: Both sisters are in their early twenties. They have a very close, friendly relationship.

FIRST INVITATION: One sister invites the other to go jogging this morning.

SECOND INVITATION: The other sister invites the first to ride bicycles this afternoon.

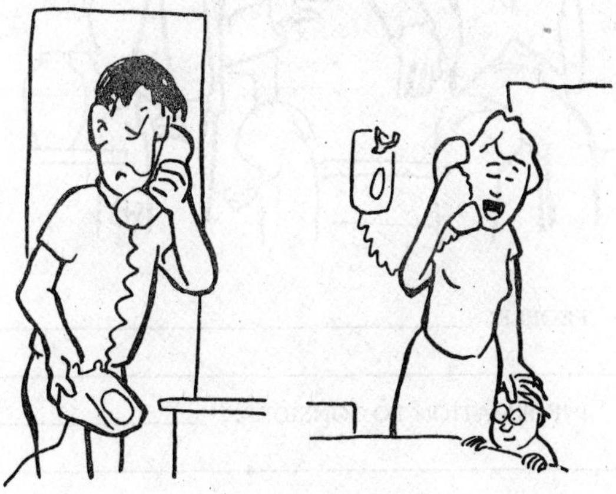

PEOPLE: A man and a woman.

INFORMATION TO CONSIDER: Both the man and the woman are middle-aged. They have only talked on the phone one time. They don't know each other very well. A mutual friend has arranged for them to go out on a blind date. The man is calling the woman on the phone.

FIRST INVITATION: The man invites the woman to go sailing on his boat this Saturday.

SECOND INVITATION: The woman invites the man to come to her house for dinner on Sunday.

PEOPLE: Two classmates at the university.

INFORMATION TO CONSIDER: Both students are women. One woman is in her early twenties. The other woman is in her late forties. It is the beginning of the semester and they just met. They don't know each other very well yet.

FIRST INVITATION: One woman invites the other woman to have lunch at Burger King.

SECOND INVITATION: The second woman invites the first to have dinner at the university coffee shop.

PEOPLE: Two next-door neighbors.

INFORMATION TO CONSIDER: Both neighbors are in their sixties and both are men. They have known each other for ten years and are close friends as well as neighbors.

FIRST INVITATION: One neighbor invites the other to go to a scary movie on Thursday night.

SECOND INVITATION: The other neighbor invites the first to go to a scary movie on Sunday afternoon.

PEOPLE: Two salespeople at a furniture store.

INFORMATION TO CONSIDER: Both salespeople are middle-aged men. They have worked with each other for five years. They are very good friends and often get together socially.

FIRST INVITATION: One person invites the other to play a game of golf tomorrow morning.

SECOND INVITATION: The other person invites the first to get a beer after work today.

PEOPLE: ______________________

INFORMATION TO CONSIDER: ______________________

FIRST INVITATION: ______________________

SECOND INVITATION: ______________________

Choose the Dialogue

1. Following are two conversations. Find a partner to help you practice them. Before you begin, cover up your partner's side of the dialogue.
2. Person A begins the conversation by reading 1. Person B chooses one of the replies in 2 and reads it to Person A.

3. Person A then reads the appropriate answer in 3. (There is only one correct response.)
4. Continue the conversation. It's very important to listen to what your partner says.

person a	***person b***
1. Do you want to get a cup of coffee with me?	***2.*** Sure, that sounds great. Where? or Thanks for asking, but I have to study. I'm writing a composition for English class tomorrow.
3. Downstairs. There's a coffee machine in the lobby. or That's too bad. Oh, by the way, I'm having a party tomorrow. Would you like to come?	***4.*** I'd like to, but I'm already busy. I'm taking my little brother to the movies. But how about doing something next Tuesday? We have the day off.* or How about going to that new restaurant next door instead? They have great desserts there.
5. Sure, that sounds like fun. Do you want to go to the library with me after we eat? We could study together for our exam next Friday. or Sure, that sounds great. How about going to the movies?	***6.*** OK. That's a good idea but I can't study too late. or OK. Give me a call on Monday night so we can decide which movie to see.

* *To have the day off* means to have a vacation from school or work.

Rotation Activity

1. If you could invite *a world leader* to do something, whom would you invite?

   ____

   What would you invite that person to do?

   ____

2. If you could invite *a famous musician* to do something, whom would you invite?

   ____

   What would you invite that person to do?

   ____

3. If you could invite *a famous actor* to do something, whom would you invite?

 ____

 What would you invite that person to do?

 ____

4. If you could invite *a famous actress* to do something, whom would you invite?

 ____

 What would you invite that person to do?

 ____

5. If you could invite *a famous athlete* to do something, whom would you invite?

 ____

 What would you invite that person to do?

 ____

directions:

1. Find a partner. Together choose one of the famous people you listed.
2. You play yourself; your partner plays the famous person.
3. Make your invitation to the famous person.
4. Have the famous person turn it down and explain why. (Remember to turn down the invitation as that famous person would.)
5. The famous person then invites you to do something on a different day. (Remember to make the kind of invitation you think that famous person would make.)
6. Repeat steps one thru five. Take turns being the famous person.

Avoiding Invitations

Sometimes you find yourself in a situation in which you don't want to or can't accept or turn down an invitation. In English there are several ways to avoid immediately accepting or refusing an invitation. Here are some of those expressions. They can be used in both formal and informal contexts.

I'll have to think about it and let you know.

I don't know what my plans are yet. Let me get back to you.

I'm not sure if I can. I'll let you know *soon* (tonight, tomorrow, in an hour...).

I'll have to check with my *roommate* (boss, secretary, boyfriend, wife...).

One-Liners

1. Find a partner and choose one of the conversation lines.
2. Together create a conversation around that line.
3. Present your role play to the group.

conversation 1

LINE: "How about going to the zoo with me this weekend?"

PEOPLE: Two women who work together in a department store.

SITUATION: Both people are crazy about animals. One woman invites the other to go to the zoo to see the new exhibits there.

conversation 2

LINE: "Thanks for asking, but maybe some other time. I have to go to the dentist this afternoon to get a tooth filled."

PEOPLE: Two friends who get together occasionally socially.

SITUATION: One friend sees the other at the grocery store. He or she invites the other person to play tennis. The other person has to decline the invitation because of a dentist appointment.

conversation 3

LINE: "I don't know what my plans are yet. Let me get back to you."

PEOPLE: Two men who work together in an office. They have a close, friendly relationship.

SITUATION: One man invites the other to spend the weekend in the woods in his cabin. The two men frequently go up to the cabin to go fishing, swimming, boating, and so on.

conversation 4

LINE: "I'd be delighted. It would be a great chance for me to see how your company operates."

PEOPLE: Two business executives who have a purely business relationship. They both work for different corporations.

SITUATION: Two business executives meet at a conference. One person invites the other to visit his or her company next week to see how it operates. The other person would really like to go.

conversation 5

LINE: "Thank you for asking, but I'm afraid I can't. I have to work tomorrow night."

PEOPLE: Two people at a party. One person is a man; the other is a woman. Both people are middle-aged. They just met and don't know each other well.

SITUATION: The woman asks the man if he wants to go to a movie tomorrow night. He declines the invitation because he has to work.

conversation 6

LINE: "I'm not sure if I can. I'll let you know this afternoon."

PEOPLE: Two classmates who are very good friends.

SITUATION: Class has just finished. One friend invites the other to go jogging between classes.

Thinking on Your Feet

1. Think of three invitations and write them down on three small pieces of paper.
2. Show the invitations to your teacher. Then put them in a container in the middle of the room.
3. To begin, one person takes a piece of paper out of the container and reads the invitation aloud to someone else.
4. That person gives an appropriate reply. He or she can either accept the invitation, turn it down, or try to avoid it.
5. Take turns so that everyone has a chance to make an invitation.

COMMUNITY EXERCISES

Invite an English-speaking friend to do something this weekend. It can be as informal as getting a cup of coffee with a roommate or as formal as dining at a very nice restaurant. After you invite the person, answer the following questions:

1. Whom did you invite? ______________________
2. How did you make the invitation (over the phone, in person . . .)? ______________________
3. What did you invite the person to do? ______________________
4. Write your invitation here: ______________________
5. Did the person accept, decline, or avoid the invitation? What exactly did he or she say? ______________________

Tonight watch television for at least one hour. Try to find examples of invitations that are made on television shows. Are the invitations accepted? Are they refused? Write down the information you hear on the following chart. The best kinds of shows to watch are situational comedies, situational dramas, or soap operas. Briefly discuss these types of television shows with your teacher. You might want to list on the board the names of a few situational comedies, situational dramas, and soap operas. Ask your teacher if you have any questions about whether or not a specific program would be useful.

	example	*one*	*two*
What was the title of the T.V. program? What type of program was it?	"The Odd Couple" A situational comedy	______ ______	______ ______
What types of people were involved in the invitation scene?	Two men who share an apartment	______ ______	______ ______
Was it a formal or an informal situation?	Informal situation	______	______
How did the person make his or her invitation?	"Hey Felix, do you want to go to the game tonight?"	______ ______	______ ______
Did the other person accept or refuse the invitation? What expression did he or she use?	He declined the invitation. "I'm too tired, Oscar. Go without me."	______ ______	______ ______
Did the other person avoid the invitation? What expression did he or she use?	No.	______ ______	______ ______
Did you hear any new expressions for inviting or accepting/declining an invitation?	"*Why don't we* get something to eat?	______ ______	______ ______

PUTTING IT TOGETHER

If you've learned this chapter well, you should now be able to: (1) make an invitation; (2) accept an invitation; (3) decline an invitation; and (4) avoid an invitation in a variety of situations. The following activities give you a chance to put these skills together and to review what you learned in the first two chapters.

Supply an appropriate question or response in each of the following spaces:

1. ______________________?	Not too bad. How about you?
2. ______________________?	No, it's nice to meet you, Paul.
3. Would you like to go to the concert with us, Mrs. Jackson?	______________________
4. ______________________?	I'd be delighted.
5. Look at the time! I've got to go.	______________________
6. ______________________?	I'm fine, thank you. How are you?
7. ______________________	It's a pleasure to meet you, too, Mr. Fowler.
8. How about going to Miami with me?	______________________
9. It was nice talking to you again.	______________________
10. ______________________	Bye-bye. See you tomorrow.
11. ______________________?	I'm sorry, but I can't. I have to work this evening.
12. ______________________?	Sure, that sounds great.
13. Mr. Smith, I'd like you to meet Dr. Thompson.	______________________
14. ______________________?	I don't know what my plans are yet. Let me get back to you.
15. I don't think we've met. My name's Bill Walsh.	______________________
16. How do you do, Father Carey?	______________________
17. Thank you for your time, Ms. Smith.	______________________

Role Plays

directions:

1. Following are several role-play situations. Find a partner and together choose a role play that interests you.
2. Read the *Situation and Setting* sections carefully. Decide together which expressions, forms of address, and nonverbal body language are most appropriate for your roles.
3. Pay special attention to details and props. This makes your role play more realistic and fun. A list of details to consider is included in each role play.

4. Practice your conversation several times. When you feel comfortable with your conversation, present it to the class.
5. Before you begin, give some details of the players, their relationship to each other, and the situation and setting.

1. SITUATION AND SETTING: A man and woman are sitting next to each other at a party. They are both bored. The woman introduces herself to the man and they have a brief conversation using small-talk topics. After a while the man invites the woman to go to a bar for a drink. She declines the invitation. They talk for a few more minutes and then the woman leaves the party because it's getting late.

PLAYERS: A man and a woman who don't know each other are at a party. They are both in their twenties. The man works for a local newspaper. The woman is getting her master's degree in business administration.

DETAILS TO CONSIDER:

Your names	Your topics of conversation
Forms of address	The reason for declining the invitation
Party setting	Nonverbal body language

2. SITUATION AND SETTING: A woman is a secretary in a very large company. One of the company's sales representatives walks into her office and greets her. They don't know each other very well, but they carry on a conversation for a few minutes using small-talk topics. The man invites the woman out on a date, but she declines the invitation. He keeps asking her out for dates on different nights. At first she tries to avoid the invitations and then she begins to turn them down. Finally, she says goodbye and leaves abruptly to avoid his continual invitations.

PLAYERS: A secretary and a sales representative who work in the same company.

DETAILS TO CONSIDER:

Your names	An office setting
Forms of address	Your topics of conversation
The name of your company	Several different invitations and replies

3. SITUATION AND SETTING: One person is a student; the other person is the student's former English professor. They meet each other by accident in a book store. They greet each other and then talk for a while. The teacher invites the student to go out to lunch next Wednesday. The student has to decline the invitation because he or she is going back to his or her country. The two people say goodbye to each other and then leave. (This is a long-term goodbye.)

PLAYERS: An English professor and a former student.

DETAILS TO CONSIDER:

Your names	Book-store setting
Forms of address	Nonverbal body language
Your topics of conversation	Long-term goodbyes

4. SITUATION AND SETTING: One person just moved into an apartment; the other person has lived in that building for many years. The long-time resident comes over to the new tenant's apartment and introduces himself or herself. The new tenant invites the other person into his or her apartment, and they talk for a while using some small-talk topics. The long-time resident then invites the new tenant to come over to his or her apartment in a couple of hours for dinner. The new tenant avoids the invitation at first, but the neighbor asks him or her again. This time the new tenant accepts. The long-time resident leaves to go home and start cooking dinner.

PLAYERS: There are two residents in an apartment. They are both men or both women. One person has lived there a long time; the other person just moved into the apartment building.

DETAILS TO CONSIDER:

Your names	Apartment setting
Forms of address	Nonverbal body language
Your topics of conversation	Avoiding an invitation

Sticky Situations

Discuss these situations together.

1. You are talking with a group of your friends. You want to invite only one of them to do something tonight. What should you do?
2. You turned down someone's invitation several times, but he or she keeps insisting that you go out. What should you do?

CHAPTER 4

APOLOGIES
CONDOLENCES

- Making and Accepting Apologies
- Offering and Accepting Condolences

Making and Accepting Apologies

You can apologize by saying:

I beg your pardon.	↑ formal
Please accept my apologies.	
Please excuse me.	
Please forgive me.	
I'm (really) (so) (very) sorry.	
I'm sorry *I broke your glasses* (I forgot your name, I'm late . . .).	
Sorry!	informal ↓

You can accept an apology by saying:

Don't worry about it.
That's all right.
That's OK.
No problem.

FOR A BETTER UNDERSTANDING

Generally speaking, North Americans do not directly accept apologies. For example, they rarely, if ever, accept apologies by saying:

Yes, I forgive you.
Yes, I accept your apology.
Yes, I excuse you.

These kinds of replies are considered to be extremely formal or condescending. When someone makes this kind of reply in English, it appears that he or she is superior to the person making the apology. To avoid this awkward situation, North Americans use phrases which seem to "dismiss" the apology. For example:

No problem.
Don't worry about it.

If you want to accept someone's apology in English, it is important to make a reply. If you say nothing, you are really telling that person that you do not accept his or her apology. For this reason, it is a good idea to learn a couple of the just-listed responses to apologies so that you can easily use them at a moment's notice.

CONVERSATION PRACTICE WITH A FRIEND

1. Find a partner and practice these two conversations aloud.
2. Switch roles for extra practice.

Person A: Oh, please excuse me. I accidentally spilled my coffee on your seat.
Person B: Don't worry about it. I can wipe it up with my handkerchief.

PEOPLE: Two men at a play. It is intermission.*

INFORMATION TO CONSIDER: Both men are middle-aged. They are sitting next to each other at the theater. They have never met each other.

REASON FOR APOLOGY: One man accidentally spilled his coffee on the other man's chair.

* An *intermission* is the free time between the acts of a play, movie, or concert.

Person A: I'm really sorry I missed your party last night. I had to work.
Person B: That's OK. I hope you can come next time.

PEOPLE: Two women who live next door to each other.

INFORMATION TO CONSIDER: Both women are in their twenties. They grew up together in the same neighborhood and are very good friends.

REASON FOR APOLOGY: One friend missed the other friend's party to which she had been invited.

Now You Try It

1. Read the following situations.
2. Find a partner and practice the apologies aloud.

PEOPLE: A doctor and a patient.

INFORMATION TO CONSIDER: The doctor is a man in his early sixties. The patient is a man in his thirties. The patient has gone to this doctor for several years. Their relationship, however, is strictly professional. They only see each other at the doctor's office when the patient has a medical problem.

REASON FOR APOLOGY: The patient forgot to go to his doctor's appointment yesterday.

PEOPLE: Two classmates.

INFORMATION TO CONSIDER: One student is a man; the other is a woman. They are both in their thirties. They often talk together in class; however, they do not socialize outside of class.

REASON FOR APOLOGY: One student borrowed the other student's class notes to copy and forgot to bring them back.

PEOPLE: A mother and a son.

INFORMATION TO CONSIDER: The son is in his early teens. He still lives at home. He has a close relationship with his mother.

REASON FOR APOLOGY: The mother asked her son to get some milk and bread at the grocery store on his way home from school. When he walks in the door and sees his mother, he realizes he forgot to go to the grocery store.

PEOPLE: A married couple.

INFORMATION TO CONSIDER: The husband and wife are middle-aged. They have a very close relationship.

REASON FOR APOLOGY: The wife yelled at her husband for playing the stereo too loudly. Now she wants to apologize for the unkind things she said.

PEOPLE: Two brothers.

INFORMATION TO CONSIDER: One brother is eighteen and the other is twenty-one. They both still live at home and have a very close relationship.

REASON FOR APOLOGY: When one brother borrowed a shirt from the other one, he tore a hole in it. Now he wants to apologize for his carelessness.

PEOPLE: ______________________

____

INFORMATION TO CONSIDER: ______________________

____

____

____

REASON FOR APOLOGY: ______________________

____

____

____

One-Sided Dialogue

1. Read the following dialogue. Only Person A's lines are given.
2. Fill in the dialogue for Person B. Read Person A's lines carefully. They give you hints about what Person B is saying.
3. When you complete the dialogue, practice it with someone.

This is a conversation between two good friends who go to the same school. They are between classes.

A: Hi (partner's name). How's it going?

B: ______________________?

A: Fine, thanks. I'm really sorry I didn't call you last night like I promised. I was watching a movie on the T.V. and forgot about the time.

B: ______________________

____

A: Would you like to go to a jazz concert with me tonight? I have an extra ticket.

B: ______________________

____

A: I understand. I have a lot of studying now, too. Instead of going to the concert, maybe we can do something this weekend.

B: ______________________

______________________?

A: Sure, I'd love to. I really love horror films—the scarier, the better. Oh, by the way, did you remember to ask your roommate if I could borrow her tape recorder?

B: ______________________

____

A: No problem. I'll call tonight and ask her myself.

B: ______________________

A: I have to go, too, or I'm going to be late for class. Bye-bye.

B: ______________________

____

Mix and Match

stores

1. A dry cleaners
2. A grocery store
3. A department store
4. A drugstore
5. A hardware store
6. A florist
7. A record shop
8. A liquor store
9. ________________

reasons for the apology

1. You forget your checkbook and can't pay for your purchases.
2. You bump into someone in the store and make him or her drop something.
3. You break something in the store.
4. You accidently take someone else's packages thinking they are yours.
5. You are drinking a can of soda and spill it on something in the store.
6. Your little child tries to take something from the store without paying for it. The manager catches him or her.
7. You brought your pet into the store. The manager tells you that no animals are allowed inside the store.
8. ________________

directions:

1. Find a partner. Together choose one Store and one Reason for the Apology around which you can create a role play. (You can choose your own if none of these interests you.)
2. Complete the following information:

   Your store name is: ________________

   Your reason for the apology is: ________________

   ____

   The people in your role play are: ________________
3. Practice your role play several times.
4. When you know it, present your role play to the group. Before you begin, tell the others the name of your store, the reason for the apology, and the players in your role play.

Offering and Accepting Condolences

Some of the expressions used in apologies are also used in condolences. When used in condolences, however, they have a different meaning. Condolences express sympathy or sorrow about someone's misfortunes. For example, when someone's relative dies, when someone loses a job, or when someone has to have an operation, we often express sympathy.

You can express sympathy by saying:

Please accept my sympathy. (formal)	
I was (so) (very) sorry to hear that ...	
It's such a shame that ... (formal/ informal)	your uncle died.
I'm (very) sorry that ... (formal/ informal)	you were fired.
It's (really) awful that ...	your trip was canceled.
What a *pity* (shame)! (formal/informal)	
I'm (so) (very) sorry ...	
That's *too bad* (terrible, awful, a shame) ...	

Some replies:

Thank you for your concern.	↑ formal
Thank you. I appreciate it.	
Thank you (very much).	
Thanks (a lot).	
Thanks. It was just one of those things.*	
Thanks. These things happen.*	informal ↓

*These two expressions are not appropriate as replies when expressing sympathy about a serious situation such as a death, a grave illness, or a bad accident.

FOR A BETTER UNDERSTANDING

If the person to whom you are speaking mentions a misfortune, you can express sympathy by saying:

Please accept my sympathy.
What a pity.
I'm (so) (very) sorry.
That's too bad.

For example:

Person A: I just heard that my aunt died.
Person B: Oh, I'm very sorry.

If you want to express sympathy about something that has not yet been mentioned in your conversation, you can use one of the following expressions:

I was (so) (very) sorry to hear that	
It's such a shame that...	your car was stolen.
I'm (very) sorry that...	you lost your job.
It's (really) awful that...	you broke your arm.

For example:

Person A: I'm sorry that your aunt died.
Person B: Thank you very much.

CONVERSATION PRACTICE WITH A FRIEND

1. Find a partner and practice these two conversations together.
2. Switch roles for extra practice.

Advisor: I was very sorry to hear that you didn't get accepted into Harvard University.
Student: Thank you very much, Dr. King. Since I didn't get accepted, I've decided to apply to several other universities.

Person A: I just found out that I can't go home during the semester break.
Person B: That's terrible! I'm really sorry.
Person A: Thanks. I'm disappointed but these things happen.

PEOPLE: A college student and his academic advisor.

INFORMATION TO CONSIDER: The advisor has counseled this student during his last semester in college and has tried to help him get into a graduate program. The student has only seen his advisor four or five times. Their conversations are friendly but somewhat formal. The professor is a middle-aged woman and the student is a man in his twenties.

REASON FOR CONDOLENCE: The advisor just learned that the student did not get accepted into Harvard's physics program.

PEOPLE: Two classmates studying English at an English language institute in the U.S.

INFORMATION TO CONSIDER: One person is a middle-aged man. The other person is a young man in his early twenties. They have become very good friends at the institute. They often socialize together outside of class.

REASON FOR CONDOLENCE: The young man just found out that he doesn't get to go home to his country during the semester break.

Now You Try It

1. Read the following situations.
2. Find a partner and practice the condolences.

PEOPLE: A young employee and his boss' wife.

INFORMATION TO CONSIDER: The woman is in her late fifties. The man is in his early thirties. These two people do not know each other. This is the first time they have ever talked to each other.

REASON FOR CONDOLENCE: The man's boss broke his back and is in the hospital. The young man is calling his boss' wife to express his sympathy about the accident.

PEOPLE: A young man and a young woman.

INFORMATION TO CONSIDER: Both the young man and woman are in their late teens. They are dating each other. They have a very close, friendly relationship.

REASON FOR CONDOLENCE: The girlfriend just found out that her boyfriend did very poorly on the TOEFL exam. He feels very bad about it.

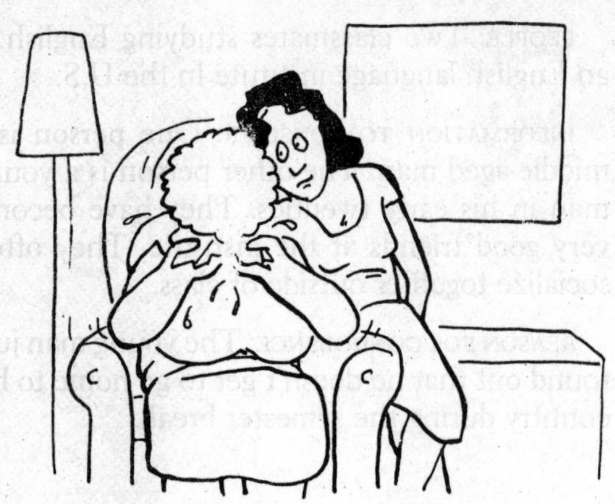

PEOPLE: Two women.

INFORMATION TO CONSIDER: One woman is in her seventies. The other woman is in her late twenties. They live next door to each other in the same apartment. They do not know each other very well. The have only greeted each other a couple of times.

REASON FOR CONDOLENCE: The woung woman found out that the older woman was robbed last night. She wants to express her sympathy to the older woman.

PEOPLE: ______________________________

____

INFORMATION TO CONSIDER: ______________

____

____

REASON FOR CONDOLENCE: _______________

____

____

PEOPLE: A daughter and a mother.

INFORMATION TO CONSIDER: The mother is in her late sixties. The daughter is in her early forties. They do not live near each other, but they still have a very close relationship.

REASON FOR CONDOLENCE: The mother has lost an antique watch that has been in their family for many years. She is very upset about it.

PEOPLE: A man and a woman.

INFORMATION TO CONSIDER: Both people work in the business department of a large store. They are both middle-aged and have worked together for several years. They are very good friends and their families often socialize together.

REASON FOR CONDOLENCE: The man just found out that he is being transferred to a store in another city. He and his family don't want to move. The woman wants to express her sympathy.

A Rotation Activity

In this activity, everyone in the class works at the "Fun Food" candy factory. It is Friday afternoon and the weekly factory meeting has just finished. All the workers are still sitting around the table. This has not been a good week for the workers. Everyone has had some bad news. Each worker and his or her problem are listed here:

1. Mr. Jamison (the boss) found out his wife is divorcing him.
2. Sam Stevenson's (the factory manager) house burned down.
3. Mary Meyers' (the receptionist) cat was hit by a car.
4. Len Levison's (the janitor) girlfriend married another man.
5. Bob Parker (a candy maker) was fired from his job at the factory.
6. Christy Lovett (a candy maker) had six teeth pulled.
7. Ben Garett (the accountant) owes $1000 in taxes.
8. Carolyn Wood's (the sales representative) stereo and T.V. were stolen.
9. LeRoy Brent (the delivery person) was not given his raise by the boss.
10. Diane White's (a secretary) husband has to have an operation next week.

directions:

1. Choose one of the characters just listed to role play.
2. Make a name tag for yourself so that everyone knows your name.
3. Imagine that the meeting just ended. You didn't get a chance to talk to anyone before the meeting. Circulate around the table and talk to at least three people. In your conversations use greetings, small talk, condolences, and conversation closings. Be sure to express sympathy about the person's particular problem. For example, you might say to the boss:
   Mr. Jamison, I heard your wife is divorcing you. I'm very sorry.
4. The person to whom you made the condolence must give you an appropriate reply. For example, Mr. Jamison might reply:
   Thank you for your concern. I really appreciate it.

What Would You Say?

Here are several lines from possible conversations that might require some type of condolence or a reply to a condolence. Give an appropriate answer to each one. You can do this exercise as a class, in pairs, or individually.

1. I heard that you broke your ankle getting off the bus. That's terrible!
   Reply: ______________________________
2. I was very sorry to hear that your brother was hurt in the car accident.
   Reply: ______________________________
3. You failed your exam? That's too bad.
   Reply: ______________________________

4. ______________________________

Thank you for your concern. I'm sure I'll feel much better by tomorrow.

5. ______________________________

Thanks, it was just one of those things. I knew I didn't have a very good chance of winning when I entered the race.

6. I'm having a lot of trouble with my visa status. I may have to go home next week.

Reply: ______________________________

7. It's a shame that you didn't get that job you wanted.

Reply: ______________________________

8. I was in a bad accident and my car was completely wrecked.

Reply: ______________________________

9. ______________________________

Thanks a lot. When my purse was stolen, I lost my driver's license.

10. My sister just told me that your grandmother died. Please accept my sympathy.

Reply: ______________________________

COMMUNITY EXERCISE

Sometime this weekend go to a place where it is very crowded. For example, you could ride on a crowded bus or subway, you could go to a crowded grocery store or movie lobby, or you could visit a crowded shopping center. Sit or stand somewhere for approximately one hour and watch the people. Listen for different examples of apologies and then answer the following questions:

1. Where did you go? How long did you stay there? ______________________________
2. Briefly describe one interesting situation in which you heard an apology. Was it a formal or an informal situation? ______________________________
3. What types of people were involved in the apology? ______________________________
4. How did one person apologize? Write the apology here. ______________________________
5. What reply did the other person make? Write the reply here. ______________________________
6. Did either person make any nonverbal gestures during the apology or reply? ______________________________
7. Did you notice a situation in which you thought someone should have apologized but didn't? Explain. ______________________________

8. Did you notice a situation in which someone apologized, but the other person made no reply? Explain.

9. Approximately how many apologies did you hear while you were there?

Watch T.V. for at least an hour. Try to find examples of condolences on the television programs. How does the person express his or her sympathy? How does the other person reply? The best kinds of programs to watch are situational dramas, dramatic movies, or soap operas. Sometimes television commercials also have examples of condolences. Ask your teacher if you have any questions about whether a specific program would be useful.

	one	*two*
What was the title of the T.V. program? What type of program was it?		
What types of people were involved in the condolence scene?		
Was it a formal or informal situation?		
Was the condolence for a very serious or minor incident?		
How did the person express his or her sympathy?		
How did the other person reply? What expressions did he or she use?		

PUTTING IT TOGETHER

If you've learned this chapter well, you should now be able to: (1) apologize; (2) accept an apology; (3) offer condolences; and (4) acknowledge a condolence in a variety of situations. The following activities give you a chance to put these skills together and to review what you learned in the first three chapters.

Mix and Match

1. Column A lists sixteen statements. Column B lists possible replies.
2. Find a partner. One person picks a statement from column A and reads it aloud.
3. The other person picks an appropriate reply from column B and reads it aloud. (In some cases, there may be more than one appropriate reply.)
4. Continue until you have read all sixteen statements. Switch roles several times.

column a	*column b*
1. Would you like to take a drive with me in the country?	Great! How about you?
2. Hello Professor Gibson. How are you today?	That's terrible. I'm really sorry.
3. Well, I've got to go now. See you later.	Sure, that sounds like fun. Thanks for asking.
4. My dog was hit by a car last night.	It's nice to meet you, too.
5. I'm sorry I forgot to give you the money I owed you. I'll write you a check right now.	I'd love to, thanks.
6. Do you want to go to the beach with us?	Good, thank you. How are you?
7. Hi. How's it going?	No problem. I know you didn't mean it.
8. Did you remember to pay the phone bill last week?	Thanks a lot. I was really counting on getting it.
9. It's a pleasure to meet you, Ms. Taylor.	Yes, that would be very nice. Thank you for asking me.
10. I beg your pardon ma'am. Are you all right?	Thank you. I appreciate it. His death was very sudden.
11. Sally, this is Bruce.	Pleasure to meet you.
12. Please accept my sympathy. He was such a nice person.	OK. Bye-bye.
13. Please forgive me! That was a stupid thing to say.	Sure, that sounds great.
14. How about going downtown with me?	Don't worry about it. It's really not that important.
15. It's such a shame you didn't get the promotion you wanted.	That's OK. I wasn't watching where I was going.
16. Hi. My name's (your name).	Oh, I'm sorry. I completely forgot.

Build-Up Role Plays

Create your own role play as a class using the following directions. Repeat the build-up process to create other role plays.

FIRST PERSON: Choose the functions which you want to use in the role play. Select them from this list:

Introducing Others/Yourself	Invitations	Accepting/Declining/ Avoiding Invitations
Greetings	Apologies	
Small Talk	Condolences	Goodbyes/Conversation Closings

SECOND PERSON: Give a setting for the role play.

THIRD PERSON: Create a role-play situation in that setting, including the players.

FOURTH PERSON: Name the important details to consider to make the role play realistic, including information about the players.

FIFTH, SIXTH, SEVENTH . . . (AS MANY AS NECESSARY) PERSON: Act out the role play.

Sticky Situations

Discuss these situations together.

1. You just apologized to someone for something you did, but the other person will not accept your apology. What should you do?
2. You just learned that a coworker you don't know very well was just fired from his or her job. You're afraid that if you mention the situation, the other person might be embarrassed. However, you're afraid that if you don't mention it, the other person will think you are rude or just don't care. How would you handle this situation?

CHAPTER 5

GRATITUDE
COMPLIMENTS
CONGRATULATIONS

- Gratitude
- Compliments and Congratulations
- Nonverbal Congratulations

Gratitude

You can express gratitude by saying:

Thank you (very much).*	That was very kind of you.
	How thoughtful of you.
	I'm very grateful.
Thanks (a lot).	I really appreciate it.
or	
Thank you (very much)* for . . .	giving me a ride.
	your help today.
	coming tonight.
	the flowers.
Thanks (a lot) for . . .	taking me to the movies.

* *Thank you very much* is considered more formal than *Thanks a lot.*

You can reply by saying:

(It was/is) my pleasure.	↑ formal
(I was/am) glad to do it.	
You're welcome.	
Don't mention it.	
No problem.	
Any time.	↓ informal

FOR A BETTER UNDERSTANDING

That was very kind of you.
How thoughtful of you.
I'm very grateful.
I really appreciate it.

These expressions are generally used to express strong gratitude to someone. Otherwise North Americans usually just say, "Thank you very much" or "Thanks a lot." Look at the difference between these two conversations:

Person A: Thanks a lot for helping me study for this exam. I really appreciate it. I don't understand anything.

Person B: No problem. I'm glad to do it.

Person A: Here's your hamburger and french fries, ma'am.

Person B: Thanks a lot.

CONVERSATION PRACTICE WITH A FRIEND

1. Find a partner and practice these two conversations aloud.
2. Switch roles for extra practice.

Person A: Thank you very much for seeing me without an appointment, Dr. Jansen.

Person B: You're welcome, Mrs. Stewart. I'm sorry your teeth are hurting.

PEOPLE: A dentist and a patient.

INFORMATION TO CONSIDER: Both the dentist and the patient are middle-aged. The dentist is a man and the patient is a woman. Mrs. Stewart has been Dr. Jackson's patient for a few years, but their relationship is strictly professional.

THANK YOU: Mrs. Stewart has a bad toothache. Dr. Jackson said that she could see him right away without an appointment. She is very grateful.

Person A: Thanks for giving me a ride home. I hate to take the bus!

Person B: Glad to do it. It was nice to have a chance to talk.

PEOPLE: Two coworkers.

INFORMATION TO CONSIDER: These two people work together in an office. One coworker is a middle-aged woman. The other is a man in his late twenties. They have a friendly working relationship but don't socialize away from the office.

THANK YOU: The man gave the woman a ride home from work. She is very grateful because she doesn't like to ride the bus.

Now You Try It

1. Read the following situations.
2. Find a partner and practice them together.

PEOPLE: Two good friends.

INFORMATION TO CONSIDER: The two friends are women in their early twenties. They have been close friends for several years.

THANK YOU: One friend gave the other a record album she really wanted for her birthday.

PEOPLE: The owner of a dry cleaners and a customer.

INFORMATION TO CONSIDER: Both the store owner and the customer are middle-aged men. The two men don't really know each other. Their only conversation is to greet each other when the customer brings in clothes.

THANK YOU: The owner of the dry cleaners cleaned the customer's suit very quickly so it would be ready for a party tonight. The customer is very grateful.

PEOPLE: A police officer and a woman.

INFORMATION TO CONSIDER: Both the police officer and the citizen are women. They don't know each other at all.

THANK YOU: The citizen was lost and the police officer gave her directions. Now she wants to thank the police officer.

PEOPLE: A grocery-store employee and a customer.

INFORMATION TO CONSIDER: The customer is a woman in her sixties. The employee is fourteen years old. He puts groceries in bags and carries them to the car. The two people don't know each other.

THANK YOU: The young man carried the customer's groceries to the car. She is very grateful for his help.

PEOPLE: Two good friends.

INFORMATION TO CONSIDER: Both friends are middle-aged men. They have been good friends for many years.

THANK YOU: One friend gave the other two tickets to a baseball game because he can't use them. The other friend really appreciates his offer.

PEOPLE: ______________________

INFORMATION TO CONSIDER: ______________________

THANK YOU: ______________________

What Would You Say?

1. You're in a crowded bus after a long day at work and you're very tired. Someone gets up and gives you his seat. You sit down and say:

2. A good friend just gave you a sweater that she knitted for you. You put on the sweater and say:

3. You've just returned a checkbook to someone you don't know. He left it in the bank where you work. He is very grateful and has thanked you several times. You say to him:

4. You are very sick with a cold. A friend comes over to your apartment and brings you your favorite magazine. When she sits down on the bed and gives you the magazine, you say:

5. Your mechanic spent all day working on your car so that you can leave tonight on a trip. You walk into the garage and say to the mechanic:

6. You are walking along the sidewalk. You see an old woman lose her balance and fall down. You help her and she thanks you for your assistance. You reply:

____

____

7. You're meeting your date for lunch at a restaurant. When you walk in, your date says, "Hey, you look great!" You reply:

____

____

8. You helped a friend fix his leaky faucet. He has just finished thanking you. You say to him:

____

____

9. It's the first day of classes, and you can't find your classroom. A teacher helps you by showing you where your room is. Before you go into the room, you say to the teacher:

____

____

10. Your friends invited you to their house for dinner. It was a delicious meal and you had a great time. When it's almost time for you to go, you turn to your friends and say:

____

____

One-Liners

1. Find a partner and choose one of the following conversation lines.
2. Together create a conversation around that line.
3. Present your role play to the group.

conversation 1

LINE: "Thank you very much. I'm very grateful! I can't believe how quickly something terrible like that can happen."

PEOPLE: A person who lives in an apartment and a firefighter.

SITUATION: The person in the apartment is cooking and a grease fire starts in the kitchen. He or she calls the fire department. A firefighter comes right away and puts out the fire before too much damage is done. The person who owns the apartment is very grateful.

conversation 2

LINE: "Thanks a lot. It's always more fun doing this when a friend helps."

PEOPLE: Two close friends.

SITUATION: One person just moved into a new house. The other person is helping him or her paint the living room. The first person really appreciates all the help he or she is getting.

conversation 3

LINE: "No problem. I was planning to go there anyway."

PEOPLE: Two next-door neighbors who are good friends.

SITUATION: One person is going to the drugstore. That person stops by his or her neighbor's apartment to see if the neighbor needs anything. The neighbor asks the first person to buy some cough medicine. He or she is very grateful because he or she is sick and doesn't feel like going to the store. The first person says it's no problem.

conversation 4

LINE: "It was my pleasure, sir/ma'am. Please let me know if I can be of assistance in the future."

PEOPLE: A very wealthy customer and a car salesperson for very expensive cars.

SITUATION: A wealthy customer just bought a very expensive car from a car dealership that sells imported cars. The customer loves the car and thanks the salesperson for helping him or her with the purchase. The salesperson responds very politely. (Their entire conversation is quite formal.)

conversation 5

LINE: "Hey, any time. What are friends for?"

PEOPLE: Two very good friends in their midthirties.

SITUATION: Two friends have been out together all evening. One friend walks the other home. When they get to the door, they both hear strange noises inside the house. One friend asks the other to come inside and look around because he or she is afraid. There is no one in the house and the first friend, embarrassed, thanks the other for looking around. The other friend says that he or she would do it "any time."

conversation 6

LINE: "Thank you very much for giving me this opportunity. I won't disappoint you."

PEOPLE: A boss and a new employee.

SITUATION: The boss of a large business just hired a new employee to work in the business office. This is the new employee's first job and he or she is very grateful. The new employee thanks the boss very much for giving him or her this chance.

Compliments and Congratulations

A compliment is a flattering remark used to express praise, respect, affection, or admiration to a person. It is difficult to rank compliments in order of informality. The formality of each expression depends on the context of the situation and the tone of your voice.

You can compliment someone by saying:

What a nice . . .	apartment.
Those are/That's a (really) nice . . .	haircut.
I really like your . . .	jacket.
You have a (really) nice . . .	English composition.
Your ________ is/are (really) nice.	puppy.

You can use many different adjectives in place of *nice*—for example, *wonderful, great, fantastic, beautiful,* and so on.

You can reply by using these expressions of gratitude:

Thank you (very much).	formal ↑	It's nice of you to say so.
		I'm flattered.
		I'm glad you like it/them.
Thanks (a lot).	informal ↓	You've made my day!

A congratulatory expression is used to indicate happiness about a person's success or good fortune.

You can congratulate someone by saying:

I'd like to offer my congratulations.		formal ↑
I'd like to offer my congratulations on . . .	your new job. / your promotion.	
Congratulations!		
Congratulations on . . .	your new job. / your promotion.	
I'm very happy for you.		
That's great.		informal ↓

You can use many different adjectives in place of *great*—for example, *wonderful, fantastic, nice,* and so on.

You can reply by using these expressions of gratitude:

Thank you (very much).*   Thanks (a lot).

* *Thank you very much* is considered more formal than *Thanks a lot.*

FOR A BETTER UNDERSTANDING

It's nice of you to say so.
I'm flattered.
I'm glad you like it.
You've made my day!

When replying to compliments, North Americans generally use these expressions to indicate strong gratitude. Otherwise they usually just say, "Thank you very much" or "Thanks a lot." Look at the difference between these two conversations:

Person A: You have beautiful children. I really like both of them.

Person B: Thank you. It's so nice of you to say so.

Person A: Hey, I like your new coat.

Person B: Thanks a lot.

CONVERSATION PRACTICE WITH A FRIEND

1. Find a partner and practice these two conversations aloud.
2. Switch roles for practice.

Person A: This is really a delicious dinner. Person B: Thank you very much. I'm glad you like it.

Person A: I graduated from college last semester. Person B: That's great! Congratulations. Person A: Thanks a lot. It's great to be finished.

PEOPLE: A boss and a new employee.

INFORMATION TO CONSIDER: Both the boss and the employee are women. The boss is middle-aged and the new employee is in her early twenties. The new employee has only worked at the company two weeks. She and her boss have a friendly relationship but they don't know each other well yet.

COMPLIMENT: The new employee invited her boss to come to dinner. The boss thinks the meal is delicious.

PEOPLE: Two acquaintances.

INFORMATION TO CONSIDER: One of the people is a man; the other is a woman. Both are middle-aged. They met each other at the university when they were both taking evening classes there. They had a friendly relationship at school but didn't socialize together. This is the first time they have seen each other in several months.

CONGRATULATIONS: The two friends run into each other on the street. One person said that she graduated from the university last semester. The other person is very happy for her.

Now You Try It

1. Read the following situations.
2. Find a partner and practice them together.

PEOPLE: Two cousins.

INFORMATION TO CONSIDER: Both cousins are women. One cousin is in her late twenties. The other is in her forties. They have a very close, friendly relationship.

CONGRATULATIONS: The younger woman just had her first baby. Her cousin is calling her on the telephone to congratulate her.

PEOPLE: A sister and a brother.

INFORMATION TO CONSIDER: Both the sister and brother are middle-aged. They live in different cities but have a very close, loving relationship.

COMPLIMENT: The brother has come to visit his sister. They haven't seen each other for a year. In that time the brother lost thirty-five pounds. The sister is complimenting her brother on how good he looks.

PEOPLE: Two very close friends.

INFORMATION TO CONSIDER: Both friends are eighteen-year-old men. They have gone to school together for the last twelve years.

CONGRATULATIONS: One friend just found out that he has been accepted to the college to which he applied. His friend is very happy for him.

PEOPLE: Two neighbors.

INFORMATION TO CONSIDER: Both neighbors are in their early fifties. They have lived next to each other for several years; however, they don't know each other very well. They talk when they see each other outside, but they don't socialize together.

COMPLIMENT: One neighbor just finished painting his house. The other neighbor comes over to his yard to tell him how good the house looks.

PEOPLE: Two coworkers.

INFORMATION TO CONSIDER: One coworker is a sixty-year-old man. The other is a woman in her twenties. The two people only see each other at work. They have a friendly but professional relationship.

CONGRATULATIONS: The man just heard at the office that the young woman is planning to get married next month. He wants to congratulate her.

PEOPLE: ______________________________

____

INFORMATION TO CONSIDER: __________

____

____

____

____

COMPLIMENT/CONGRATULATIONS: ______

____

____

____

Thinking on Your Feet

1. Think of a compliment you could make to someone in your class. Write it here:

   ____

2. Think of some success or good fortune you've recently had for which someone could congratulate you. Write it here:

   ____

3. Take turns reading your statements to each other. The person to whom you make your statement must give an appropriate answer.
4. Keep playing until everyone has had a chance to read both statements.

Rotation Role Play

This role play is acted out in groups of eight. Pretend that everyone is a small-business owner who belongs to your city's Association of Small-Business Owners. You have been members for several years and know each other quite well. Tonight you are having your monthly social meeting, which is a time when you can get together to talk about business problems and your personal lives.

directions:

1. Choose to be one of the characters listed on the following chart. Make a name tag with your name and the name of your company.
2. At the meeting, talk to several other members. In each conversation use greetings, small talk, a congratulation (see column A), a compliment (see column B), conversation closings, and goodbyes.
3. During each conversation also discuss one big problem you are having with your business. (You can decide what the problem is.) If the person to whom you are talking can help you with your problem, thank him or her. If the other person can't help you, have him or her apologize and explain why.

The Members of the Association of Small-Business Owners

	a. congratulate him/her because...	*b. compliment him/her because...*
1. Harold Carter	He won first place in a tennis tournament.	He got a nice hair cut.
2. Brenda Kline	She quit smoking.	She got a beautiful tan in the Bahamas.
3. Peter Moore	He opened a new store last month.	He is wearing a very nice suit tonight.
4. Alice Stone	Today is her wedding anniversary.	She is wearing a beautiful pearl necklace.
5. Harry Parker	His daughter just graduated from law school.	He grew a beard and it looks nice.
6. Donna Mann	She got married two weeks ago.	The homemade cake she brought to the meeting is delicious.
7. Luis Torres	He just bought a new home.	He speaks English very well.
8. Vicky Martin	The govenment gave her business a big loan.	She is much thinner than the last time you saw her.

Nonverbal Congratulations

In addition to verbal expressions, North Americans sometimes also use nonverbal body language when offering congratulations. When we congratulate someone using nonverbal body language, we use our bodies instead of words. This helps emphasize our happiness at that person's good fortune. Everyone uses nonverbal body language when speaking. However, the specific manner in which it is used varies from culture to culture.

Here are some important features of nonverbal congratulations:

- Facial Expressions
- Handshaking
- Patting on the Arm or Back
- Hugging
- Kissing

Discussion Activity

Discuss these questions together. When answering these questions, consider how the age, gender, status, and relationship of the people might affect your responses.

1. Generally speaking, what kind of facial expressions do North Americans have when offering congratulations? Are they reserved? Do they smile a lot?
2. How do North Americans shake hands when offering congratulations? Do they always shake hands? In which situations are people most likely to shake hands?
3. Demonstrate how North Americans might pat someone on the arm or back. Do they always pat someone's arm or back when offering congratulations? When are they most likely to do so?
4. When might North Americans hug or kiss someone when offering congratulations?
5. How is nonverbal body language used to offer congratulations in your country? Would any of the uses of nonverbal body language previously mentioned be considered impolite or silly in your country? Explain.
6. Have two people volunteer to act out the following situations. Use only nonverbal body language; do not speak.

SITUATION ONE: You are both classmates. One of the classmates has just told the other that she (or his wife, if a man) is going to have a baby. You have a friendly relationship but don't know each other very well. You really only talk before and after each class. How would you congratulate the person who is going to have a baby?

SITUATION TWO: You are two very close family members. One person just told the other that she (or his wife, if a man) is going to have a baby. How would you congratulate the family member?

As a group, discuss which nonverbal body language was used in each congratulation. How were the congratulations the same? How were they different?

NONVERBAL ROLE PLAYS

Following are five situations in which someone is offering congratulations to another person. After you read each one, indicate whether the situation is formal or informal by circling the appropriate response.

Explain how you would use body language in each situation. Be sure to state how the following factors affected your decision: age, gender, status, and relationship of the people in the role play.

situations:

1. One good friend just told another friend that he or she got a big promotion at work. The two people are approximately the same age and have a very close relationship.

   formal *informal*

   Appropriate nonverbal body language: ______________________

   ____

2. A student just told a former professor that he or she was hired for his or her first job. The two people have a friendly but professional relationship.

   formal *informal*

   Appropriate nonverbal body language ______________________

   ____

3. A boyfriend just told his girlfriend that he won $25,000 in a big contest.

   formal *informal*

   Appropriate nonverbal body language: ______________________

   ____

4. An employee just heard that his or her boss won first place in a citywide chess tournament. The employee wants to congratulate his or her boss. They have a friendly but professional relationship.

   formal *informal*

   Appropriate nonverbal body gestures: ______________________

   ____

5. One coworker just told another that he or she has accepted a job offer to become the president of a new company. The two coworkers have a close, friendly relationship.

   formal *informal*

   Appropriate nonverbal body gestures: ______________________

   ____

directions:

1. Find a partner and together choose one of the roles.
2. Choose roles and create a conversation using appropriate language expressions and nonverbal body language.
3. Pay special attention to the age, gender, status, and relationship of the people in the role play.
4. Practice the conversation together. Use anything in the room as props.
5. When you know the conversation, present it to the group. Before you begin, give a brief explanation of your role play.
6. After you present your role play, have the others discuss how you used nonverbal body language in your congratulations.

Look at the following photographs. Discuss how nonverbal body language is being used in each congratulation. Do you think each interaction is formal or informal? Why?

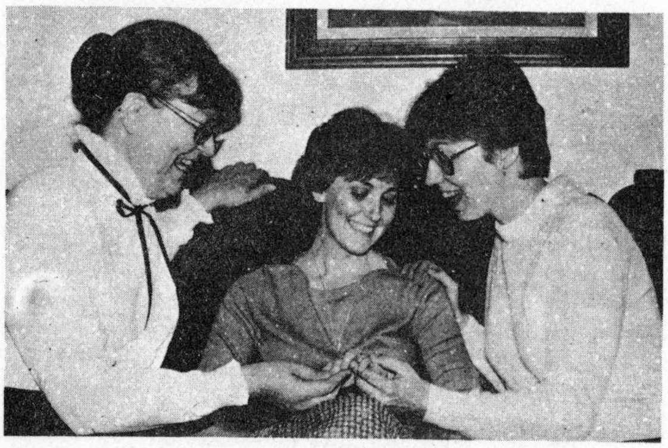

Photograph taken by Jim Farley.

1. ______________________________

____

____

____

Photograph taken by Jim Farley.

2. ______________________________

____

____

____

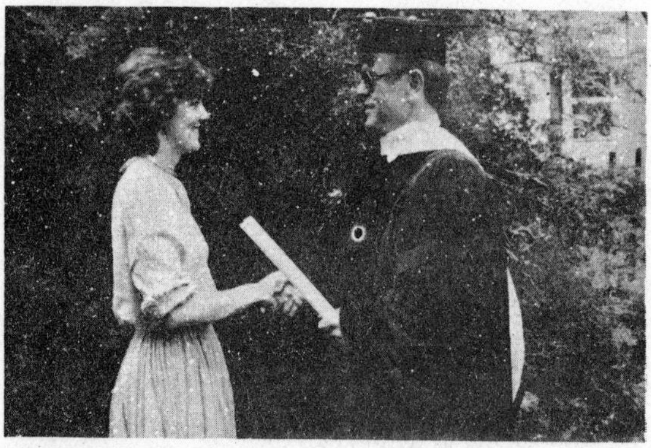

Photograph taken by Haissam Chehab.

3. ______________________________

____

____

____

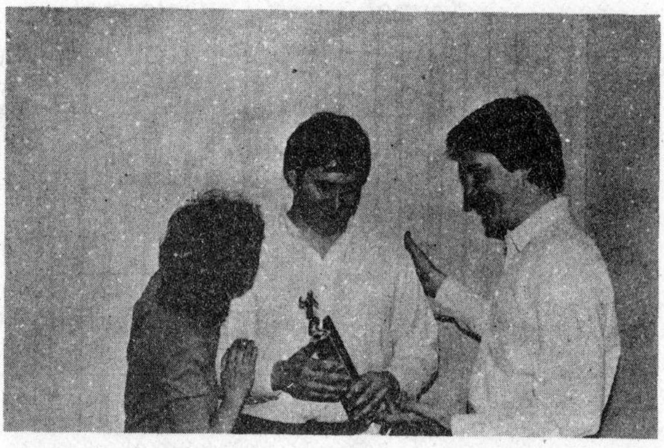

Photograph taken by Teresa Farley.

4. ______________________________

____

____

____

COMMUNITY EXERCISES

This weekend you are going to put yourself in several situations in which you thank people or listen to thank yous. Several questions for you to answer follow each activity listed here.

1. Call an airline office and ask how much it costs to fly one-way to any city you choose. When the ticket agent gives you the information, thank him or her.

questions:

A. To which city did you ask to fly? ______

B. How much did it cost? ______

C. Did you consider the conversation to be formal or informal? ______

D. How did you thank the ticket agent? Write it here: ______

E. What reply did the ticket agent give you? Write it here: ______

2. Buy something at a drugstore. When the cashier finishes helping you, thank him or her.

questions:

A. What did you buy at the drugstore? ______

B. How did you thank the cashier? Write it here: ______

C. What reply did the cashier give you? Write it here: ______

D. Did you consider the conversation to be formal or informal? ______

3. Go to an expensive department store. Watch and listen to someone buying something.

questions:

A. What did the customer buy? ______

B. Approximately how old were the customer and the salesperson? Were they men or women? ______

C. Did the customer thank the salesperson? Write what the salesperson said here: ______

D. What reply did the salesperson give to the customer? Write it here: ______

E. Did you consider their conversation to be formal or informal? ______

4. Ask for directions to somewhere in the city. When the person gives you the directions, thank him or her.

questions:

A. Briefly describe the person you asked for directions (regarding age, gender, and relationship to you). ______

B. To where did you ask the person to give you directions? ______

C. How did you thank the person? Write it here: ______

D. What reply did he or she give? Write it here: ______________________

____

E. Did you consider the conversation to be formal or informal? ________

____

5. Go to a restaurant. Watch and listen to the customers for at least an hour. Try to listen to people's expressions of gratitude and their replies.

questions:

A. To what type of restaurant did you go (a fast-foods restaurant, an expensive restaurant, a sandwich shop, and so on)? ______________

____

B. In your opinion, did the customers thank the waitresses or waiters for their help:

most of the time some of the time not very often

C. In your opinion, did the waitresses or waiters reply appropriately to the customers' expressions of gratitude:

most of the time some of the time not very often

D. Did you consider the conversation between the waitresses or waiters and the customers to be generally formal or generally informal? ______________________________

E. What were some of the expressions of gratitude and replies that you heard in the restaurant? List some of them here:

expressions of gratitude	*replies*
____________	____________
____________	____________
____________	____________
____________	____________
____________	____________
____________	____________
____________	____________

Compliment three English-speaking people and then answer the following questions:

	first person	*second person*	*third person*
Whom did you compliment (your mother, a friend, a classmate . . .)	____________	____________	____________
For what did you compliment that person?	____________	____________	____________

	first person	second person	third person
How did you compliment that person? Write your compliment here.			
How did the other person respond? Write it here.			
Did you consider the conversation to be formal or informal?			

Offer congratulations to three English-speaking people and then answer the following questions. (It may be a little difficult to find three people, but it is good practice if you can.)

	first person	second person	third person
Whom did you congratulate (your brother, a classmate . . .)?			
For what did you congratulate that person?			
How did you congratulate that person? Write it here.			
How did the other person respond? Write it here.			
Did you use any nonverbal body language? Explain.			
Did you consider the conversation to be formal or informal?			

PUTTING IT TOGETHER

If you've learned this chapter well, you should be able to: (1) thank someone; (2) give a compliment; and (3) offer congratulations in a variety of situations. The following activities give you the opportunity to review these skills as well as the information from the first four chapters.

In this activity, give either an appropriate question or statement for each blank.

example

That's a beautiful sweater!	Thanks a lot. I just bought it.
Here's the sandwich you ordered.	Thank you very much.
1. What a beautiful home!	______
2. I just got a new job that pays $18.00 an hour.	______
3. ______	Thank you for your concern. It was just one of those things.
4. My daughter was married this weekend.	______
5. ______	I'd love to. What time will you pick me up?
6. Good morning, Dr. Weiss. How are you today?	______
7. Here's my car, Paul. Use it as long as you need to.	______
8. I'm sorry, Mr. Price. I completely forgot about our appointment.	______
9. ______	Thanks a lot. I'm glad you like it.
10. Alison, do you know Henry?	______
11. ______	I have to go too. Bye-bye.
12. Congratulations! You really deserve this raise.	______
13. You look very nice this evening, honey.	______
14. ______	I'd love to but I can't. I have a very important meeting this evening.
15. Look at the time! I have to go now.	______
16. ______	Thank you very much. I'm really grateful.
17. Hello. My name's Elizabeth Jones.	______
18. Thank you for the great birthday present. I love it!	______
19. ______	That's all right. Just hand in the assignment by tomorrow morning.
20. ______	Thank you very much.

Role Plays

directions:

1. Following are several role-play situations. Find a partner and together choose a role play that interests you.
2. Read the *Situation and Setting* sections carefully. Decide together which expressions, forms of address, and nonverbal body language are most appropriate for your roles.
3. Pay special attention to details and props. This makes your role play more realistic and fun. A list of details to consider is included in each role play.
4. Practice your conversation several times. When you feel comfortable with your conversation, present it to the class.
5. Before you begin, give some details of the players, their relationship to each other, and the situation and setting.

1. SITUATION AND SETTING: A person just won a two-week vacation to a tropical island. That person is talking with a close friend who is offering congratulations on his or her good luck. They are both at a restaurant having lunch. The person going on the trip asks the close friend to watch his or her home while he or she is away. The vacationing person is very grateful because the close friend says he or she will take care of everything. During the conversation each person also makes a compliment to the other. The role play ends with the two friends' paying their check and leaving the restaurant.

PLAYERS: Two friends who are very close. They are both middle-aged.

DETAILS TO CONSIDER:

Your names

The name of the island to which you are going

A restaurant setting

Exact details of what the close friend is going to care for

Your compliments

Nonverbal body language

2. SITUATION AND SETTING: Today is one person's birthday. Two friends are helping that person celebrate it. They each give that person a birthday present which he or she can wear (for example, a hat, jacket, or watch). The person celebrating the birthday is very grateful and happy about the gifts. He or she tries them both on and the friends compliment him or her on how good the gifts look. During the conversation, one of the three friends announces that he or she is engaged to be married. The other two are very surprised and offer their congratulations. The conversation closes when the three people end the party and go home.

PLAYERS: Three good friends who are are in their early twenties. They have known each other for several years.

DETAILS TO CONSIDER:

Your names

The party location

The birthday gifts

Which person is getting engaged

Nonverbal body language

3. SITUATION AND SETTING: Two close family members are talking to each other. One family member tells the other that he or she was finally able to buy a house. The other family member excitedly congratulates him or her. The person who's moving asks if the other person would be available to help with the move. That person says he or she will do anything, for which the other person is very grateful. During the conversation, the person who is moving shows pictures of the new home. The other family member compliments him or her on how beautiful it is. The conversation ends when they leave each other to go to their own apartments.

PLAYERS: Two family members who have a close relationship. They do not live in the same house.

DETAILS TO CONSIDER:

Your relationship to each other	Photographs
Your names	Nonverbal body language
The location where you are talking	

4. SITUATION AND SETTING: Two employees just heard that the boss' son got his first job. It is a great job, and he'll make a lot of money. They greet the boss in the hall and then congratulate him or her. While they are talking, the boss asks each of the employees to stay late to work on a special project that must be finished by tomorrow. When they say they will stay, the boss is very grateful. During the conversation, each person makes a compliment to someone. The conversation ends when the boss says it's time to get back to work.

PLAYERS: A boss and two employees of a business. The boss is fifty-five years old. The two employees are in their late twenties or early thirties.

DETAILS TO CONSIDER:

Your names	The type of special project for the two employees
The name of your business	The compliments made to each other
Office hallway setting	
The type of job the boss' son got	

Sticky Situations

Discuss these situations together.

1. Someone just thanked you *sarcastically* instead of gratefully. How should you reply?
2. A person just complimented or congratulated you insincerely. How should you reply?

CHAPTER 6

REQUESTS
COMMANDS
WARNINGS
DIRECTIONS

- Requesting Others to Do Something
- Warnings, Commands, Directions
- Negative Request Forms

Requesting Others to Do Something

A person uses requests to ask someone to do something that will benefit him or her. Requests commonly used in English are listed here:

Would you be kind enough to . . .	↑ formal	
Would you (please) . . .		lend me five dollars?
Could you (please) . . .		drive me to school?
Could you possibly . . .		help me with my homework?
Do you think you'd be able to . . .		repeat that question?
Will you (please) . . .		go to the store for me?
Can you (please) . . .	informal ↓	

You can reply affirmatively by saying:

It would be my pleasure.	↑ formal
I'd be glad to.	
Certainly.	
Of course.	
Yes.	
All right.	
Sure.	
OK.	informal ↓

You can reply negatively by using one of the expressions here. These can be used in both formal and informal situations.

(No, I'm sorry)	I'm afraid not. I can't.	(and excuse)

You can also make a request by saying:

	lending me five dollars?
	driving me to school today?
Would you mind . . .	helping me with my homework?
	repeating that question?
	going to the store for me?

To accept someone using this request form, you can say:

No.	It would be my pleasure.	formal
	I'd be glad to.	
	Not at all.	
	I wouldn't mind.	
	I don't mind.	
	Of course not.	informal

To turn down someone using this request form, use the expression here. It can be used in both formal and informal situations.

(I'm sorry) I can't.	(and excuse)

FOR A BETTER UNDERSTANDING

Requests beginning with "Would you mind . . ." are a little different from the other request forms on page 108. When you want to accept this kind of request, you say "No." For example:

Person A: Would you mind turning off the fan?
Person B: No, not at all.

In conversational English, you often hear people accepting this request by saying "Yes." For example:

Person A: Would you mind turning off the fan?

Person B: Yes, of course.

Although affirmative replies are *grammatically* incorrect, they are perfectly acceptable in conversational English.

As when refusing an invitation (see Chapter Three), North Americans usually give some explanation why they are refusing a request. For example:

Person A: Would you help me with my homework tonight?

Person B: I'm sorry but I can't. I have a big chemistry exam tomorrow that I have to study for.

In English it is considered impolite or a little abrupt to just reply, for example, "No, I can't."

CONVERSATION PRACTICE WITH A FRIEND

1. Find a partner and practice these two conversations aloud.
2. Switch roles for extra practice.

Person A: Would you please bring me another cup of coffee?

Person B: Certainly, sir. I'd be glad to.

Person A: Could you also sit down and talk for a few minutes?

Person B: No, I'm sorry, but I can't. I have to wait on the other customers.

Person A: Would you mind babysitting for my little brother tonight? I'm supposed to watch him, but I need to study for a big exam.

Person B: No, of course not. I'd be glad to babysit for you.

Person A: Could you possibly babysit tomorrow too?

Person B: No, I'm sorry. I can't. I have a date tomorrow.

PEOPLE: A waitress and a customer.

INFORMATION TO CONSIDER: The waitress is a young woman in her late teens. The customer is a man in his early sixties. He has come to this restaurant several times, but the waitress doesn't know him.

FIRST REQUEST: The customer would like another cup of coffee.

SECOND REQUEST: The customer would like to talk to the waitress for a few minutes.

PEOPLE: Two roommates.

INFORMATION TO CONSIDER: Both roommates are twenty-year-old men. They are in college and share an apartment together. They have only known each other for a few weeks, but they have a friendly relationship.

FIRST REQUEST: One roommate wants the other to babysit for his little brother tonight.

SECOND REQUEST: He wants his roommate to babysit for his little brother tomorrow also.

Now You Try It

1. Read the following situations.

2. Find a partner and practice the requests using the previous conversations as models.

PEOPLE: A shoe salesperson and a customer.

INFORMATION TO CONSIDER: The shoe salesperson is a twenty-one-year-old man. The customer is a man in his late forties. The two men don't know each other.

FIRST REQUEST: The customer wants to try on a pair of loafers.

SECOND REQUEST: The customer also wants the salesperson to show him a pair of tennis shoes, but the salesperson doesn't have any left.

PEOPLE: A bank teller and a tourist visiting the city.

INFORMATION TO CONSIDER: The bank teller is a woman in her late twenties. The tourist is a man in his early fifties. The tourist is not a regular customer at this bank. The teller and the customer don't know each other.

FIRST REQUEST: The tourist would like the bank teller to make change for his fifty-dollar bill.

SECOND REQUEST: The tourist would like the teller to cash his check. This isn't possible because he doesn't have an account at the bank.

PEOPLE: A hairdresser and a client.

INFORMATION TO CONSIDER: The hairdresser is a man in his twenties. The customer is a woman in her early forties. The woman often has her hair cut by this man. They have a friendly but professional relationship.

FIRST REQUEST: The client would like the hairdresser to cut her hair very short.

SECOND REQUEST: The client would also like him to dye her hair blonde. He can't dye her hair because he is too busy today.

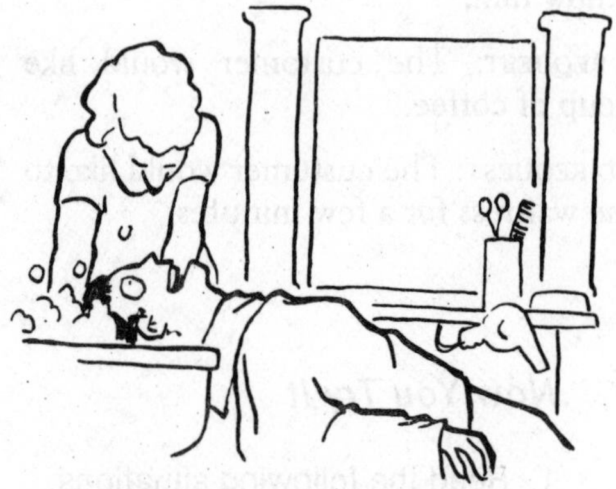

PEOPLE: A husband and a wife.

INFORMATION TO CONSIDER: Both people are in their twenties. They have a very close relationship.

FIRST REQUEST: The husband would like his wife to buy some wine on her way home from work.

SECOND REQUEST: He would also like her to fill up the car with gas on her way home from work. She can't, however, because she forgot her credit card this morning and she doesn't have very much cash.

PEOPLE: Two friends.

INFORMATION TO CONSIDER: One of the friends is a woman; the other is a man. They are both twenty-year-old students at a university. They have known each other for several years and have a friendly relationship.

FIRST REQUEST: The woman wants to borrow her friend's Beatles album.

SECOND REQUEST: She also wants to borrow his guitar, but he needs it to practice for a concert.

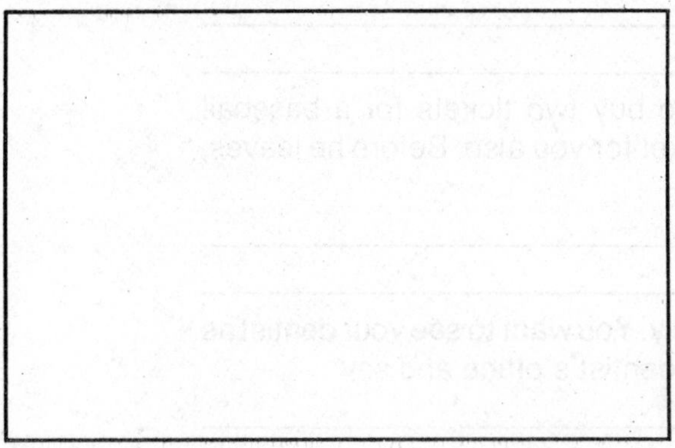

PEOPLE: ____________________

INFORMATION TO CONSIDER: ____________________

FIRST REQUEST: ____________________

SECOND REQUEST: ____________________

What Would You Say?

Make a request for each of the following situations. The first time you make the request, begin with the expression, "Would you mind..." Then make the same request again using one of the other request forms.

example

You are visiting a friend, and it is very hot in her apartment. You say to her:

A. Would you mind opening a window?

B. Could you possibly open a window?

1. There's no food in your house for dinner. You have a lot of work to do so you don't have time to go to the grocery store. You say to your roommate:

   A. ____________________

   B. ____________________

2. Your cat just had kittens and you're having a hard time finding homes for all of them. You call up your next-door neighbor and say:

   A. ____________________

   B. ____________________

3. Your friend just told you that he's going to the sports store near your house. You need some new golf balls but don't have the time to go yourself. You say to your friend:

A. ____________________

B. ____________________

4. You've been trying to open a jar of pickles for five minutes but the lid is stuck. You say to your friend sitting in the other room:

A. ____________________

B. ____________________

5. You have to move fifteen boxes in your office down to the basement. A coworker walks by your office door. You run into the hall and say to her:

A. ____________________

B. ____________________

6. Your brother is going downtown to buy two tickets for a baseball game. You'd like him to get one ticket for you also. Before he leaves, you say to your brother:

A. ____________________

B. ____________________

7. One of your teeth is hurting very badly. You want to see your dentist as soon as possible. You call up your dentist's office and say:

A. ____________________

B. ____________________

8. You are at the airport, and you can't find the gate at which your parents are arriving. You go to the information desk and say:

A. ____________________

B. ____________________

9. You are studying for a big exam, and your sister is playing her stereo very loudly. You say to her:

A. ____________________

B. ____________________

10. You are on an airplane. The flight attendant assigned you to an aisle seat, but you'd rather sit by the window. You ask the person sitting by the window:

A. ____________________

B. ____________________

Thinking on Your Feet

Think of five requests you might make to other people in your class. For example:

Do you think you'd be able to lend me a dollar?

Can you please give me a cigarette?

Would you mind giving me your phone number?

Write your requests on a piece of paper. You can make them funny or serious. Take turns making your requests to each other. (Make just one request each turn.) The person to whom you made the request has two choices:

A. ACCEPT THE REQUEST: If the person accepts the request, he or she must give an appropriate reply and actually do what the person requested. For example:

Person A: Would you please open the door? I'm really hot.
Person B: Sure, I'd be glad to. (The person then opens the door.)

B. TURN DOWN THE REQUEST: If the person turns down the request, he or she must give an appropriate reply and then explain why. For example:

Person A: Could you possibly lend me a dollar?
Person B: I'm sorry, but I can't. I don't have any money with me.

Continue playing until everyone has had at least one chance to make a request.

Warnings, Commands, Directions

In English, imperatives are often used to give *warnings, commands,* and *directions*. Here are some examples:

warnings	*directions*	*commands*
Be careful!	Heat the oven to 450°.	Turn off the T.V.
Watch out!	Turn left on Main Street.	Pay before leaving.
Don't!	Take this medicine every two hours.	Don't sit on the grass.
Run!	Plant this tree in early fall.	Be quiet.

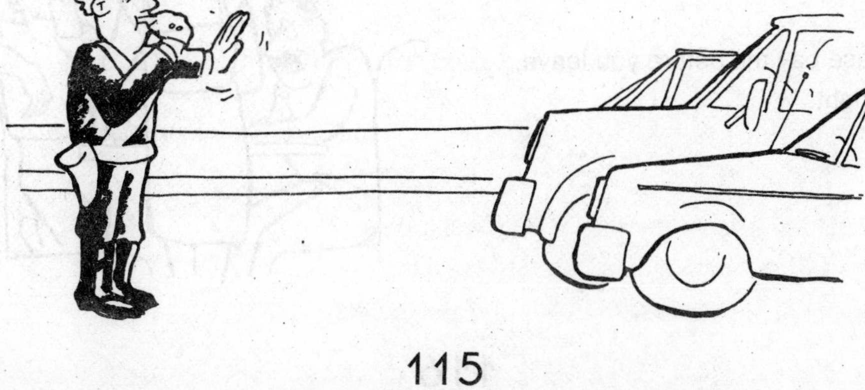

FOR A BETTER UNDERSTANDING

Warnings, commands, and *directions* differ from the other functions in this book because there are no specific replies which people generally make. Your reply (if you make one at all) is dependent on the context of the situation. Look at the following examples:

1. You might want to thank someone:

Person A: Take this medicine every two hours and your rash should be gone by tomorrow.

Person B: Thank you very much, Dr. Silver. I really appreciate it.

2. You might want to apologize:

Person A: Please turn down your stereo! We have company coming in a few minutes.

Person B: Oh, I'm sorry Dad. I didn't know anyone was home.

3. You might simply want to acknowledge the warning, command or directions:

Person A: Please pay me before you leave.

Person B: All right.

4. You might not make any reply. For example, it is very probable that no one would make a reply if your teacher made the following command to your class:

Person A: Please sit down so that we can get started.

Negative Request Forms

Negative request forms can be used as *polite commands* or *requests* (see the next section, *For a Better Understanding*). Here are some examples:

Would you mind not sitting there?	Would you mind not going there?
Could you possibly not do that?	Would you please not smoke in my house?
Will you please not bring your pet?	

FOR A BETTER UNDERSTANDING

Negative request forms deserve special attention. They usually function as *polite commands* but they can also be used as *requests* depending on the situation. Whether these forms are used as requests or commands is also very dependent on the *age, status,* and *relationship* of the people involved. As an example, look at the following sentence:

Would you mind not smoking in here?

If you walked into a room of strangers and said this, they would most likely think you were politely commanding them to not smoke. If a child said the same thing to his or her father, however, he would most likely understand it to be a request because the child would be in no position to order the father to not smoke.

Consider each of the following situations and try to decide whether they are examples of requests or commands. Circle the appropriate answer. Discuss your answers with the group.

1. A son is talking on the phone with one of his friends. His father walks into the room and starts talking to him. The son says:
   Dad, could you please not ask me questions when I'm on the phone?
   request *polite command*

2. A man knocks on his neighbor's door at two o'clock in the morning and says:

   Would you mind not playing your stereo so loudly?

   request *polite command*

3. It is the middle of a big exam. The teacher says to one of the students:

   Mark, will you please not talk during the test?

   request *polite command*

4. A student walks up to a professor after class and says:

   Could you possibly not tell anyone that I failed the exam?

   request *polite command*

5. A boss walks into an employee's office and says:

   Tomorrow, would you please not park your car so close to mine? It's very difficult for me to get out.

   request *polite command*

CONVERSATION PRACTICE WITH A FRIEND

1. Find a partner and practice these two conversations aloud.
2. Switch roles for extra practice.

Person A: Watch out! That bottle is broken.
Person B: Thanks a lot. I almost cut myself.

PEOPLE: Two friends.

INFORMATION TO CONSIDER: One person is a man; the other is a woman. The man is in his sixties. The woman is in her thirties. They have known each other for several years and have a very close relationship.

WARNING: The two friends are cooking dinner together. The woman picks up a bottle of ketchup that is broken. The man warns her that she might cut herself. The woman is grateful because she didn't know the bottle was broken.

Person A: Please be home by 10 o'clock.
Person B: Oh, all right.

PEOPLE: A parent and a child.

INFORMATION TO CONSIDER: The child is a teenager. The parent and child have a very close relationship.

COMMAND: The child is getting ready to go out with some friends. The parent tells the child to be home by 10 o'clock because she has to go to school tomorrow. The child unwillingly agrees.

Now You Try It

1. Read the following situations.
2. Find a partner and practice the *commands, warnings,* and *directions.*

PEOPLE: Two strangers.

INFORMATION TO CONSIDER: Both people are middle-aged men. They have never met each other before.

WARNING: Both men went to the park (separately) to each lunch. The city just painted all the benches with green paint. One of the men sees the other man start to sit down on one of the benches and quickly warns him. The other man is grateful because he is wearing a very expensive suit.

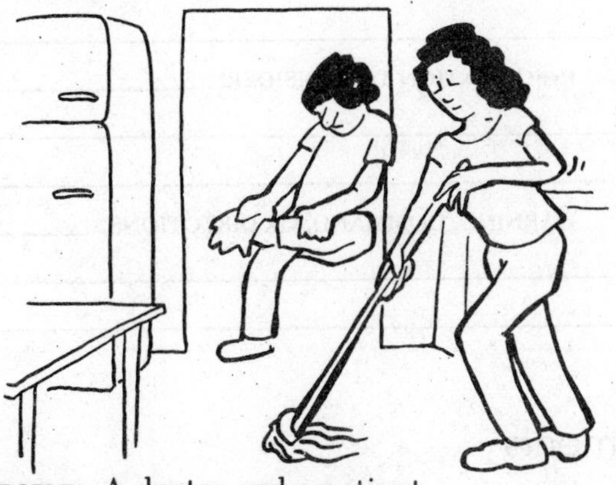

PEOPLE: A sister and a brother.

INFORMATION TO CONSIDER: The brother is nineteen years old and the sister is eighteen years old. They both live at home and have a close relationship.

COMMAND: The sister just finished cleaning the kitchen floor and she's very tired. Her brother is just about to step into the kitchen with mud all over his shoes. She tells him to wipe his feet before he comes inside.

PEOPLE: A doctor and a patient.

INFORMATION TO CONSIDER: The doctor and the patient are women in their early thirties. They have never met each other before.

DIRECTIONS: Both people are in the emergency ward of the hospital. The patient badly sprained her ankle while playing volleyball. The doctor is giving her directions on how to take care of her sprain.*

*There are two basic steps to treating a sprained ankle: (1) soak the ankle in ice water; (2) keep it elevated.

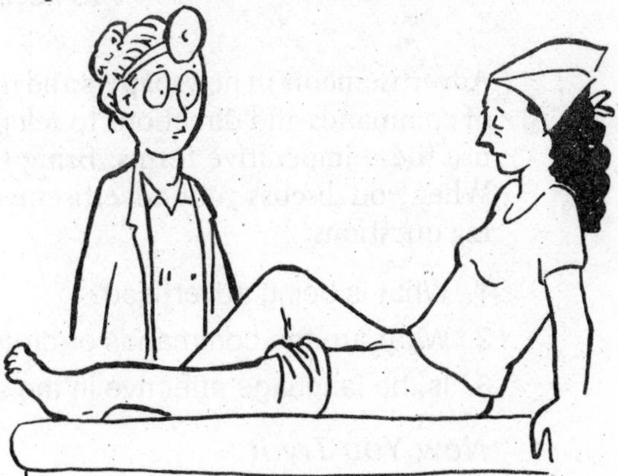

PEOPLE: A husband and a wife.

INFORMATION TO CONSIDER: The husband and wife are in their early sixties. They have a very close relationship.

WARNING: The husband and wife are standing up in their attic. When the husband starts to walk around, the boards make a very strange cracking sound. The wife warns her husband to be careful. She is afraid the floor might collapse.

PEOPLE: A bank teller and a new customer.

INFORMATION TO CONSIDER: The bankteller is a man in his late twenties. The customer is a nineteen-year-old woman. The two people don't know each other.

DIRECTIONS: The woman is opening her first checking account. She needs to endorse* the back of her check, but she doesn't know how. The teller gives her directions on how to endorse a check. The customer is grateful to the teller for showing her how to do it.

* There are two steps to endorsing a check: (1) sign your full name on the back of the check; (2) write your bank account number below your name.

PEOPLE: ______________________________

INFORMATION TO CONSIDER: ______________________________

WARNING, COMMAND, OR DIRECTIONS: ______________________________

Advertisements

Advertisements in newspapers and magazines often use the imperative form of commands and directions to sell products. Find five advertisements that use these imperative forms. Bring them to class to share with the others. When you discuss your advertisements with each other, answer the following questions:

1. What is being advertised?
2. What are the commands or directions in the advertisement?
3. Is the language effective in the advertisement? Explain.

Now You Try It

Create your own advertisement to sell one of the products listed here. (The advertisements you just discussed should give you some ideas.) Use at least three commands or directions in your advertisement. After you write your advertisement, present it to the group. If possible, have the product or a picture of your product to show while presenting your advertisement. After you present it, have the others discuss the following questions:

1. What is being advertised?
2. What are the imperatives in the advertisement?
3. Are they being used as commands or directions?

some possible products to advertise

A new kind of toothpaste
An effective bug spray
A new kind of beer
A men's cologne
A new kind of pain reliever
A new kind of sports car
A new kind of shampoo
A new kind of cigarette
A scary movie playing at a local theater
A trip to a tropical island
A new kind of potato chip or cracker
A space-age toy for children

______________________ ______________________

______________________ ______________________

Mix and Match

These role plays give you a chance to practice negative request forms to make polite commands and requests.

directions:

1. Look at the pairs of people listed here.
2. Find a partner and together choose a pair that interests you. Then choose a location in which your role play can take place.
3. Create a short conversation between these two people in which one of them makes a request or polite command using a negative request form (see page 117). In your conversation also use:
   Introductions (or greetings);
   Conversation closings and goodbyes.
4. Practice your conversation until you know it well. Use any props, name tags, and nonverbal gestures that are necessary.
5. When you know the conversation, present it to the class. Before you begin, give some details of the players, their relationship to each other, and the situation and setting.
6. At the end of the role play, have the other people try to decide, based upon the context of the situation, whether you made a negative request or a polite command.

pairs of people

1. A police officer and a citizen
2. Two executive businesspeople
3. A teacher and a student
4. A gas-station owner and a customer
5. Two people sitting on a bus
6. A parent and a child
7. Two strangers on a sidewalk
8. A librarian and a patron
9. A waitress and a customer

locations

1. At school
2. Downtown
3. At an apartment or a home
4. At a library
5. At a restaurant
6. At a shopping center
7. In a car or a bus
8. On a highway
9. At a gas station

Choose the Dialogue

1. Following are two conversations. Find a partner to help you practice one of them. Before you begin, cover up your partner's side of the dialogue.
2. Person A begins the conversation by reading 1. Person B chooses one of the replies in 2 and reads it to Person A.
3. Person A then reads the appropriate answer in 3. There is only one correct choice.
4. Continue the conversation. It's very important to listen to what your partner says.

person a	*person b*
1. Could you possibly help me fix my car? It's not working right.	***2.*** Sure, I'd be glad to. What's the problem? or I'm sorry, but I can't. I don't know anything about cars.
3. I don't either, and I have to get it fixed. Would you mind telling me the name of your mechanic? or When I start my car, the oil warning light comes on.	***4.*** Oh, that's easy to fix. I'll show you. Take off the oil cap, pour in a quart of oil, and put the cap back on. or Of course not. His name is Harry Reed. He works at the Ready-Serve gas station.
5. Will you tell me how to get there from here? or Thanks a lot for helping me do that. Now I'd like to look at the engine.	***6.*** OK. Go two blocks down Main Street and turn right. The gas station is on the corner of Main Street next to a grocery store. By the way, would you please tell Harry that I'm bringing my car to the gas station on Tuesday for a tune up? or Watch out! Don't touch the engine. It's very hot!
7. Ouch! I really burned my hand. or Sure, and don't forget about my party Saturday night. It's at 8:30.	***8.*** Thanks for reminding me. I'll come early. or Quick! Go inside and run cold water on your hand. That will stop the pain.

COMMUNITY EXERCISES

Look for examples of how the imperative form of *commands, warnings,* and *directions* are used in public. Then complete the following chart. Some places you might find these forms being used are: (1) street signs; (2) advertisements; (3) billboards; (4) cleaning products, medicine bottles, canned and frozen foods, and so on.

the phrase	*where did you find it?*
1. Do not enter	Street sign
2.	
3.	
4.	
5.	
6.	
7.	
8.	
9.	
10.	

Try to make a request to each of the people listed in the following chart. Make any request you think is appropriate for the situation you are in. Complete the chart and bring it to class so that you can share your experiences.

	what request did you make?	*what reply did the person give?*	*was the situation formal or informal?*
Your teacher			
A classmate			
Someone you don't know, such as a person on a bus			
A neighbor			
A police officer			
A salesperson			

This weekend, listen very carefully for requests. You'll hear them on the radio, on the T.V., and almost anywhere there are people (such as in restaurants, on subways, and in bookstores). Fill in the following chart for three requests you heard. Bring the filled-in chart to class so that you can share your experiences.

	first request	*second request*	*third request*
Briefly describe the situation.			
Where did you hear the request (on the phone, at the store . . .)?			
What types of people were involved in the request?			
Was the situation formal or informal?			
What was the request?			
What was the reply?			
Did you hear any request forms or replies not discussed in class? What were they?			

PUTTING IT TOGETHER

If you've learned this chapter well, you should be able to: (1) make a request; (2) accept and turn down a request; (3) give a warning; (4) make a command; and (5) give directions in a variety of situations. The following activities give you the opportunity to put these skills together and to review the information from the first five chapters.

Multiple Choice

1. Your best friend just introduced his mother to you. You shake her hand and reply:
   A. How's it going, Mrs. Ryan?
   B. Do you like all the rain we're having, Mrs. Ryan?
   C. It's a pleasure to meet you, Mrs. Ryan.
2. You walk into the kitchen. Your child is about to put his hand on a hot stove. You say to him:
   A. Would you please not put your hand on the stove? It's hot.
   B. Think before you touch! That stove is very hot.
   C. Don't touch that! It's hot.
3. You are talking with a casual acquaintance at work. When you glance at your watch, you notice that you're late for an appointment. You need to bring the conversation to a close, so you say:
   A. It's getting late. I have to go now.
   B. Goodbye.
   C. It was nice being here. Keep in touch.
4. You sit down in your seat in the nonsmoking section of an airplane. The woman sitting next to you is smoking. Cigarette smoke really bothers you, so you turn to her and say:
   A. Would you mind not smoking? This is the nonsmoking section.
   B. Put out your cigarette. This is the nonsmoking section.
   C. Please don't smoke. This is the nonsmoking section.
5. You are having a brief conversation with a friend. You just asked him, "How is your family?" A good follow-up question might be:
   A. Why isn't your daughter married yet?
   B. How does your son like college?
   C. Is your son still living with his girlfriend?
6. You're in the kitchen making an apple pie. You forget the next step of the recipe, so you ask your roommate sitting in the next room what to do. Your roommate yells back:
   A. Do you think you'd be able to cut the apples into little pieces?
   B. Cut up the apples into little pieces.
   C. Would you mind not cutting the apples into such little pieces?
7. A classmate just invited you to go to the movies Saturday night. You're not sure yet if you can go, so you reply:
   A. Yes, I'd love to. Thanks for asking.
   B. I'm sorry, but I can't. My brother is coming to visit me this weekend.
   C. I'm not sure if I can. I'll have to let you know tomorrow.
8. A husband and a wife are getting ready to go to work. As the wife walks out the door, she says:
   A. Would you mind having a nice day?
   B. Can you please have a nice day?
   C. Have a nice day.
9. You just ran into a good friend whom you see very frequently. You say to him:
   A. Hi! It's nice to meet you.
   B. Hi! How are things?
   C. Hello. It's been such a long time.

10. You're in a department store, and you want to buy a pair of shoes. You walk up to the salesperson and say:
    A. Will you please help me?
    B. Please help me.
    C. Help me, miss.
11. You are having a cup of coffee at a friend's apartment and you just accidentally spilled your coffee all over the rug. As you start to clean it up, you say:
    A. Please accept my sympathy.
    B. Oh, that's all right.
    C. I'm really sorry. Let me clean it up.
12. You see someone step out into the street in front of a car. You shout:
    A. Please watch out for that traffic.
    B. Watch out!
    C. Would you be kind enough to watch out?
13. You are staying in the hospital. When a cousin comes to visit you, she brings you a bunch of beautiful flowers. You say to her:
    A. Thanks a lot. They're beautiful!
    B. Don't mention it. I was glad to do it.
    C. Congratulations!
14. You're in your lawyer's office waiting for your appointment. The secretary walks into the room and says:
    A. Could you possibly wait fifteen more minutes, Mr. Baker?
    B. Please wait fifteen more minutes, Mr. Baker.
    C. Would you please leave now, Mr. Baker?

Build-Up Role Plays

As a class (or in small groups if the class is large), create one or several build-up role plays.

FIRST PERSON: Choose the functions to use in this role play from the following list:

- Introducing Others/Yourself (or Greetings)
- Small-Talk Topics
- Invitations
- Accepting/Declining/Avoiding Invitations
- Apologies
- Condolences
- Expressions of Gratitude
- Compliments, Congratulations
- Requests
- Warnings, Commands, Directions
- Conversation Closings/Goodbyes

SECOND PERSON: Give a setting (location) for the role play.

THIRD PERSON: Create a situation in that setting.

FOURTH PERSON: List the important details to consider to make the role play realistic. Include specific information about the players.

FIFTH PERSON, SIXTH PERSON . . . : Act out the role play.

Sticky Situations

Discuss these situations together.

1. You politely turn down a request but the other person keeps on insisting that you accept it. What can you do?
2. Someone you don't know very well commands you to do something you don't want to do. How would you handle this situation?

CHAPTER 7

OFFERS
SEEKING PERMISSION

- Offering to Do Something
- Seeking Permission

Offering to Do Something

A person offers to do something to show his or her willingness or readiness to help. Expressions commonly used in English to offer to do something are listed here. Two common general offers are: *Is there anything I can do to help?* or *What can I do to help?*

	formal ↑ / informal ↓	
May I . . .	formal	
Would you like me to . . .		help you with the dishes?
Could I . . .		do that job for you?
Can I . . .	informal	go to the grocery store for you?
I'll . . .		help you figure out that problem?

You can accept an offer by saying:

	formal ↑ / informal ↓	
If you wouldn't mind.	formal	Thank you (very much).
I'd appreciate it.		
If you don't mind.		
Please.		Thanks (a lot).
Yes.	informal	
Sure.		

You can decline an offer by saying:

	formal ↑ / informal ↓	
	formal	I appreciate your offer.
No.		That's not necessary.
		Thank you (very much) for asking.
		Thanks (a lot) for asking.
	informal	Thanks anyway.

FOR A BETTER UNDERSTANDING

When declining an offer, in addition to expressing gratitude, it's considered polite to give some kind of explanation. You can give a very general kind of explanation such as:

It's not necessary.
I think I can manage by myself.
I don't need any help.

You can also give a more specific explanation like the one in the following conversation:

Person A: Would you like me to buy the Sunday newspaper before I come over to your house?

Person B: No, thanks for asking but I already have one.

CONVERSATION PRACTICE WITH A FRIEND

1. Find a partner and practice these two conversations aloud.
2. Switch roles for extra practice.

Person A: Could I help you change that tire, miss?

Person B: Yes, thank you very much. I'm really having a hard time.

PEOPLE: Two strangers.

INFORMATION TO CONSIDER: One person is a woman in her late twenties. The other person is a middle-age man. They have never met before.

OFFER: The man sees the woman stopped on the side of the road trying to change a flat tire. He stops his car and offers to help the woman, and she gratefully accepts.

Person A: Can I set the table for you, Laura?

Person B: No, I can do it in a couple of minutes. Thanks for asking.

PEOPLE: Two close friends.

INFORMATION TO CONSIDER: Both people are middle-aged women. They have been friends for many years.

OFFER: One woman invited the other to her house for dinner. The guest offers to set the table, but the other woman declines the offer.

Now You Try It

1. Read the following situations.
2. Find a partner and practice the offers together.

PEOPLE: A salesperson and a customer.

INFORMATION TO CONSIDER: The salesperson is a man in his early twenties. He works in a very expensive men's clothing store. The customer is a man in his early sixties. The two people do not know each other.

OFFER: The customer wants to buy a wool suit. The salesperson offers to show him the different styles of wool suits the store has. The customer accepts his offer.

PEOPLE: Two apartment residents.

INFORMATION TO CONSIDER: Both of the residents are women. One woman is in her late twenties. The other woman is in her early seventies. The women have said, "Hello" to each other but don't know each other very well.

OFFER: The young woman sees the elderly woman trying to carry two sacks of groceries up the stairs. She offers to help, and the elderly woman gratefully accepts.

PEOPLE: Two roommates.

INFORMATION TO CONSIDER: Both roommates are twenty-year-old students at a college. They have known each other for two years and have a close, friendly relationship. Both men are studying for big exams.

OFFER: One roommate decides to go to a fast-food restaurant to get some dinner. He offers to get something for his roommate; however, his roommate declines because he isn't hungry.

PEOPLE: Two coworkers.

INFORMATION TO CONSIDER: One coworker is a middle-aged woman. The other coworker is a man in his early twenties. They both work for a very large company. They occasionally talk to each other but their relationship is strictly professional.

OFFER: The woman is supposed to go to the airport to meet one of the company's clients; however, she has a lot of work to do at the office. The man offers to go to the airport for her, and she gratefully accepts.

PEOPLE: Two close friends.

INFORMATION TO CONSIDER: Both friends are women in their early forties. They are next-door-neighbors and have been very good friends for many years.

OFFER: One woman's father, who lives in another city, is very ill. She is going to visit him for a few weeks. Her friend offers to keep her children for her while she is away. The other woman declines the offer because her husband has decided to stay home and take care of the children.

PEOPLE: ______________________

____

INFORMATION TO CONSIDER: ______________________

____

____

OFFER: ______________________

____

____

Thinking on Your Feet

Write an appropriate offer for each of the following situations:

1. Make an offer to someone concerning a loan (of money).

   ____

2. Make an offer to someone who is having a lot of trouble with school work.

   ____

3. Make an offer to someone whose car is not running properly.

___

4. Make an offer to someone who is afraid of being alone during a thunderstorm.

___

5. Make an offer to help someone who is very busy.

___

6. Make an offer to someone who is moving to a new house.

___

7. Make an offer to someone who has a broken leg and can't move around easily.

___

8. Make an offer to someone whose house you are at for dinner.

___

directions:

Take turns making your offers to each other. The person to whom you make the offer can either accept it or turn it down. If you turn down the offer, you must also give some kind of explanation. Continuing playing until everyone has had a chance to make several offers.

One-Liners

1. Find a partner and choose one of the following conversaticn lines.

2. Together create a conversation around that line.

3. Present your role play to the group.

conversation 1

LINE: "Could I help you carry that?"

PEOPLE: A salesperson and a customer in a department store.

SITUATION: A person just bought a television in a department store. It is big and difficult to carry. The customer tries to pick it up but has a lot of trouble. The salesperson offers to help carry it.

conversation 2

LINE: "I really appreciate your offer, but my brother already said he would help me."

PEOPLE: Two neighbors. One neighbor is middle-aged; the other is a teenager.

SITUATION: A teenager is sitting in the driveway trying to fix his or her broken bicycle. An older neighbor comes over and offers to help fix the bike. The teenager declines the offer because his or her brother already said he would help.

conversation 3

LINE: "Would you like me to do it this time?"

PEOPLE: Two good friends.

SITUATION: One friend is trying to hang wallpaper but really doesn't know what he or she is doing. The wallpaper keeps falling down or getting wrinkled. A good friend offers to help because he or she has had a lot of experience hanging wallpaper.

conversation 4

LINE: "Yes, please. Thank you very much. It's really too much work for one person."

PEOPLE: Two coworkers.

SITUATION: One person is working very late on an important report for the company. A coworker walks into the first person's office and offers to help finish the report. The first person gratefully accepts the offer because he or she thinks its too much work for just one person.

conversation 5

LINE: "Can I get anything for you while I'm there?"

PEOPLE: A grandparent and a grandchild. The grandparent and the grandchild are both North Americans.

SITUATION: The grandchild is nineteen years old and is going to take a vacation in Japan. The grandchild wants to know if he or she can get his or her grandmother anything while in Japan.

conversation 6

LINE: "Thanks for asking, but I think I can manage it by myself."

PEOPLE: Two classmates.

SITUATION: Class just ended. One person has a lot of books and notebooks to carry. Another classmate offers to help carry the things. The first classmate thanks the second but declines the offer.

Seeking Permission

A person seeks permission when he or she wants to be given the consent to do something. Expressions commonly used in English are:

formal ↑ ↓ informal	
May I (please) . . .	spend the weekend at the beach?
Would it be possible for me to . . .	miss class tomorrow?
Could I (please) . . .	call you back later?
Could I possibly . . .	bring a friend home to dinner?
Is it all right if I . . .	go shopping with you?
Can I (please) . . .	

You can grant permission by saying:

(formal ↑ ↓ informal)

By all means.
Certainly.
Of course.
Yes.
All right.
Sure.
OK.

You can deny permission by saying:

(formal ↑ ↓ informal)

No. I'd prefer that you not. (and explanation).
I'd rather you didn't.
I don't think you should.
I'm afraid not.
I don't want you to.
I'm sorry, you can't.

You can also seek permission by saying:

Would you mind if I * . . .	spend/spent * the weekend at the beach?
Do you mind if I . . .	miss/missed * class tomorrow?
	call/called * you back later?
	bring/brought * a friend home for dinner?

* The verb in the *if* clause of the sentence "Would you mind if I . . ." is identical to a past-tense form.

You can reply affirmatively to these expressions by saying:

I'd be glad for you to.	formal
Not at all.	↑
No. I wouldn't mind.	
I don't mind.	↓
Of course not.	informal

You can reply negatively by saying:

I'd prefer that you not:	formal	
I'd rather you didn't.	↑	
That's not such a good idea		(and explanation).
I don't think you should.		
I don't want you to.	↓	
I'm sorry, but you can't.	informal	

FOR A BETTER UNDERSTANDING

The expressions "Would you mind if I . . ." and "Do you mind if I . . ." are a little different from the other expressions used to seek permission. When you want to reply affirmatively to these two expressions, you say, "No." For example:

Person A: Would you mind if I called you back later?
Person B: No, of course not. (In other words: It would be fine for you to call back later.)

In conversational English, you often hear people replying to these expressions affirmatively by saying, "Yes." For example:

Person A: Would you mind if I called you back later?
Person B: Yes, of course.

Although these replies are *grammatically* incorrect, they are perfectly acceptable in conversational English.

North Americans generally give some explanation why they are refusing someone's permission to do something. For example:

Person A: Is it all right if I bring a friend home to spend the weekend?
Person B: No, I don't want you to this weekend. We have to finish painting the house and I really need your help.

CONVERSATION PRACTICE WITH A FRIEND

1. Find a partner and practice these two conversations together.
2. Switch roles for extra practice.

Person A: Could I please leave work early tonight?
Person B: Yes, it's not very busy tonight anyway.
Person A: Is it all right if I also come to work a little late tomorrow?
Person B: No, I'm sorry but you can't. We're having a big sale, so you need to be here on time.

Person A: Can I come over to your apartment tonight to study for the test?
Person B: Sure. Come whenever you'd like. I'll be home all evening.
Person A: Do you mind if I bring my dog with me?
Person B: I don't think you should. I have a cat who really hates dogs.

PEOPLE: A boss and a salesperson.

INFORMATION TO CONSIDER: They both work at a big plant store. The boss is a man in his late fifties. The salesperson is a man in his late twenties. The two men have known each other for about a year.

FIRST REQUEST FOR PERMISSION: The salesperson wants to leave work a little early tonight.

SECOND REQUEST FOR PERMISSION: The salesperson also wants to come to work late tomorrow. The boss says he can't because the store is having a big sale.

PEOPLE: Two classmates.

INFORMATION TO CONSIDER: The two classmates are both in their twenties. One of the students is a man; the other is a woman. They have been good friends for a couple of years.

FIRST REQUEST FOR PERMISSION: The man wants to know if he can come over to the woman's apartment to study for a big test.

SECOND REQUEST FOR PERMISSION: The man also wants to know if he can bring his dog with him. The woman doesn't want him to because she has a cat who hates dogs.

Now You Try It

1. Read the following situations.
2. Find a partner and practice the conversations using the preceding dialogues as models.

PEOPLE: A doctor and a patient.

INFORMATION TO CONSIDER: The doctor is a man in his late thirties. The patient is a woman in her early thirties. The doctor and patient have known each other for a few years but their relationship is strictly professional.

FIRST REQUEST FOR PERMISSION: The patient wants to know if she can stop taking the medicine the doctor gave her because she feels much better now.

SECOND REQUEST FOR PERMISSION: The patient also wants to know if she can cancel her appointment since she is feeling better. The doctor doesn't think that's a good idea because he wants to give her a checkup.

PEOPLE: An apartment manager and a new tenant.

INFORMATION TO CONSIDER: The apartment manager is a middle-aged man. The new tenant is a twenty-one–year-old man. The tenant just moved into the apartment, so he and the apartment manager don't really know each other.

FIRST REQUEST FOR PERMISSION: The tenant wants to know if he can paint his living room.

SECOND REQUEST FOR PERMISSION: The tenant also wants to know if he can remove the carpeting in the living room. The apartment manager tells him that he can't because it's a permanent part of the apartment.

PEOPLE: A teacher and a student.

INFORMATION TO CONSIDER: The teacher is a middle-aged man. The student is a woman in her early twenties. The student has taken two courses with this teacher. They have a friendly but professional relationship.

FIRST REQUEST FOR PERMISSION: The student wants to know if she can come late to class tomorrow.

SECOND REQUEST FOR PERMISSION: She also wants to know if she can hand in her assignment late. The teacher doesn't want her to because he won't have enough time to grade it.

PEOPLE: A hotel receptionist and a guest.

INFORMATION TO CONSIDER: The hotel receptionist is a man in his early thirties. The guest is a man in his early fifties. The guest is checking into the hotel for the first time.

FIRST REQUEST FOR PERMISSION: The guest wants to know if he can have another person stay in his room if he pays for it.

SECOND REQUEST FOR PERMISSION: The guest also wants to know if he can stay an extra night. The receptionist tells him that he can't because all the rooms in the hotel are already taken.

PEOPLE: Two sisters.

INFORMATION TO CONSIDER: One sister is seventeen years old; the other sister is eighteen years old. They both live at home and have a very close relationship.

FIRST REQUEST FOR PERMISSION: The younger sister wants to know if she can borrow her sister's yellow sweater.

SECOND REQUEST FOR PERMISSION: The younger sister wants to know if she can also borrow her sister's plaid skirt. The older sister tells her she can't because she is going to wear it today.

PEOPLE: ______________________________

____

INFORMATION TO CONSIDER: ______________________________

____

FIRST REQUEST FOR PERMISSION: ______________________________

____

SECOND REQUEST FOR PERMISSION: ______________________________

____

____

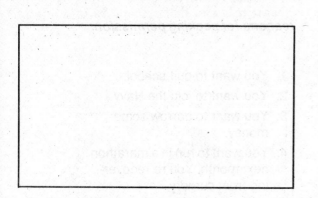

One-Sided Dialogue

1. Read the following dialogue. It is a conversation between a salesperson and a customer.
2. Complete the dialogue for the customer. Read the salesperson's lines carefully. They give hints about what the customer is saying.
3. When you have completed the dialogue, find a partner and practice it.

Salesperson: Are you going to buy that sweater, sir/ma'am?

Customer: Yes, ______________________________

Salesperson: No, I'm sorry but you can't. We don't accept credit cards at this store.

Customer: ______________________________

Salesperson: Certainly you can use your personal check. Could I please see your driver's license?

Customer: ______________________________

Salesperson: Thank you very much.

Customer: ______________________________

Salesperson: Of course. You can exchange it for any other sweater we have if your daughter doesn't like it.

Customer: ______________________________

Salesperson: No, I'm sorry. It's not possible. Our telephone is only for employees. There's a pay phone outside the front door. Would you like me to put that sweater in a box before you leave?

Customer: ______________________________

Mix and Match

person from whom you are seeking permission:

1. A parent
2. A teacher
3. A boss
4. A bank vice-president
5. A good friend
6. An academic advisor
7. A salesperson
8. A doctor
9. ______________________

reasons for seeking permission:

1. You want to quit school.
2. You want to join the Navy.
3. You want to borrow some money.
4. You want to run in a marathon next month. You're recovering from surgery.
5. You want to bring a girlfriend or boyfriend home from school.
6. You want to exchange a pair of pants because you don't like the color.
7. You want to get a face lift.*
8. You want to take a vacation.
9. You want to talk to someone about a serious problem.
10. ______________________

* A *face lift* is a type of plastic surgery which removes wrinkles from the face.

directions

1. Find a partner. Together choose one Person and one Reason for Seeking Permission around which you can create a role play. (You can choose one of your own if none of these interests you.)
2. In your conversation, the person from whom you are seeking permission can either accept or turn you down.

3. Complete the following information:

   The person from whom you are seeking permission is: ______________

   Your reason for seeking permission is: ______________

   ____

4. Practice your role play several times. When you know it, present your role play to the group. Before you begin, tell the others the roles you are playing and the reason you are seeking permission.

COMMUNITY EXERCISES

Watch TV for at least one hour this week. Try to find examples of people offering to do something for someone else. Write down the information you hear in the following chart. The best kinds of shows to watch are situational dramas or soap operas. Ask your teacher if you have any questions about whether or not a specific program would be useful.

	one	*two*	*three*
What was the title of the T.V. program? What type of program was it?			
What types of people were involved in the scene in which the offer was made (an old man, a young woman, parents, lovers . . .)?			
Was it a formal or an informal situation?			
How did the person make the offer?			
Did the other person accept or refuse the offer? What expression did he or she use?			
Did you hear any new expressions for making an offer or accepting or refusing an offer?			

Ask the following people for permission to do something. After your conversation, complete the chart.

	your teacher	*a classmate*	*your boss*	*a friend*
What were you asking permission to do?				
How did you ask for permission?				
How did the other person reply?				
Was the situation formal or informal?				

PUTTING IT TOGETHER

If you've learned this chapter well, you should now be able to: (1) offer to do something; (2) accept or turn down the offer; (3) ask permission to do something; and (4) grant or deny permission to do something. The following activities give you the opportunity to practice using these skills. You also have a chance to review the information from the first six chapters.

Mix and Match

1. Column A lists twenty statements. Column B lists twenty possible replies.
2. Find a partner. Have one person pick a statement from Column A and read it aloud. Then have the other person pick an appropriate reply and read it aloud. (In some cases, there may be more than one appropriate reply.)
3. Continue until you have read all twenty statements. Switch roles several times.

column a	*column b*
1. May I help you find something, ma'am?	a. That's all right. I think everyone at the meeting was a little angry.
2. You look great! I love your haircut.	b. No problem. I was glad to do it.
3. Would it be possible for me to exchange this red coat for that blue one?	c. Great! How about you?
4. Could you please tell me how to get to Shaker Football Stadium?	d. OK. See you later.
5. I'm really sorry I got so angry at you during the meeting.	e. Thanks a lot. I just got it cut this morning.
6. Thanks a lot for mailing those letters for me.	f. It was nice seeing you again. Goodbye.
7. I really like your new car!	g. Yes, if you wouldn't mind. I'd like to buy a silk blouse for my sister. I can't find her size.
8. Would you like me to water your plants while you're on vacation?	h. Thanks for asking, but my brother is going to do it.
9. Would you like to go to the movies tonight?	i. Of course. Bring as many friends as you'd like.
10. Could I talk to you for a few minutes? I have a problem.	j. Certainly sir. I'll put the blue one in a box for you.
11. Dr. Fields, I'd like you to meet Mr. Potter.	k. Happy to meet you.
12. Can I bring a friend to your party?	l. I'm fine, thank you. How are you?
13. Congratulations on your new job!	m. No, I'm sorry, but I can't. I just moved to the city and I don't know where it's located.
14. Can I help you do anything to get ready?	n. No, not at all.
15. Hi. Katie. How are things?	o. It's a pleasure to meet you.
16. Oh, look at the time! I have to go.	p. Sure, that sounds like fun.
17. Do you mind if I have another piece of cake?	q. Thanks a lot.
18. Dan, this is Tony.	r. I'm sorry, but I'm busy right now. Let's get together and talk tonight instead.
19. It was nice being here again.	s. Thank you very much.
20. Good afternoon, Mrs. Thompson. How are you?	t. Thanks for asking, but I'm already finished.

Role Plays

1. Following are several role-play situations. Find a partner and together choose a role play that interests you.
2. Read the *Situation and Setting* sections carefully. Decide together which expressions, forms of address, and nonverbal body language are most appropriate for your roles.
3. Pay special attention to details and props. This makes your role play more realistic and fun. A list of details to consider is included in each role play.
4. Practice your conversation several times. When you feel comfortable with your conversation, present it to the class.
5. Before you begin, give some details of the players, their relationship to each other, and the situation and setting.

1. SITUATION AND SETTING: A person was just in a single-car accident. He or she only has minor injuries but the car was totally wrecked. Another driver stops to help. That driver offers to drive the accident victim to the hospital and the victim accepts. The person who was in the accident also asks if he or she can put some boxes into the other person's car. He or she doesn't want to leave the boxes in the wrecked car while they are at the hospital. The other person says that would be fine.

PLAYERS: A person in a car accident and another driver who stops to help.

DETAILS TO CONSIDER

Your names	Car-accident setting
Forms of address	Type of injuries
Introducing yourselves	Nonverbal body language

2. SITUATION AND SETTING: A person who lives alone is very sick with a virus. A neighbor, who is a good friend, comes to visit to see how the sick person is. The neighbor offers to go to the store and buy the medicine the sick person needs, and he or she gratefully accepts. The sick person then asks if he or she can spend the night at the neighbor's house because the furnace works better. It's much warmer at the neighbor's house. The neighbor says it would be fine.

PLAYERS: A sick person and a neighbor.

DETAILS TO CONSIDER

Your names	What kinds of medicine to buy
Forms of address	Nonverbal body language
Bedroom setting with a sick person	

3. SITUATION AND SETTING: A person doesn't have enough money to pay the bills this month. A good friend is at the person's apartment. The friend offers to help the first person make a budget sometime soon so that this same problem doesn't happen next month. The other person gratefully accepts the help. The first person then asks to borrow some money until the next pay day. The good friend, however, turns him or her down because he or she also needs the money to pay bills.

PLAYERS: A person in financial trouble and a good friend.

DETAILS TO CONSIDER

Your names	What kind of bills the first person must pay
Forms of address	Nonverbal body language
Apartment setting	

4. SITUATION AND SETTING: A person has applied for a new job. The job has a good salary, job security, and a chance for promotion. Right now the person is at home with a good friend waiting for a phone call to see if he or she got the job. The person waiting for the phone call has to do some important errands. The good friend offers to stay there and wait for the phone call. The other person says that's not necessary because he or she has a machine on the phone that records messages. He or she then asks to borrow the good friend's car because his or her car is broken. The good friend gladly lets the other person borrow the car.

PLAYERS: A person waiting for a job offer and a good friend.

DETAILS TO CONSIDER

Your names	Description of the new job
Forms of address	Type of errands to be done
Apartment setting	Nonverbal body language

Sticky Situations

Discuss these situations together.

1. Imagine that you really need help doing something and a friend offers to help. However, you can tell that your friend is offering to help more out of politeness than an honest willingness to help. Should you accept or turn down your friend's offer?
2. You ask permission to do something and the person you ask hedges instead of giving you a definite answer. What should you do?

CHAPTER 8

ADVICE
INTENTIONS

- Advising Someone
- Stating Your Intention to Do Something

Advising Someone

Advising someone means counseling or making a recommendation to that person regarding a particular decision. Expressions commonly used in English to give advice are listed here. They can be used in formal and informal situations.

I (strongly) advise you to . . .	↑ strong	take some money out of the bank.
I (strongly) recommend that you . . .		look for a new job.
You (really) ought to . . . /You (really) should . . .		get a divorce.
Why don't you . . .	neutral ↓	budget your money more carefully.

You can accept someone's advice by using one of the following expressions. These can be used in formal and informal situations.

That's a good* idea.	
That's a good* suggestion.	(Thank you.)
I'll do that.	
You're right.	(Thanks.)
All right.	
OK.	

* Instead of *good,* you can say: *great, excellent, nice, wonderful.*

You can turn down someone's advice by using one of the following expressions. These expressions can be used in formal and informal situations.

That's not (such) a good idea (for me) because . . .	I don't have any money in my checking account
I'm afraid that won't help (me) because . . .	my salary at my present job is too good to give up.
I don't want to do that because . . .	
I can't do that because . . .	

FOR A BETTER UNDERSTANDING

When North Americans turn down someone's advice, they generally give some kind of explanation. For example:

Person A: Why don't you ask your boss for a raise if you need more money?

Person B: That's not such a good idea because our company is having a lot of financial problems right now.

In English it is considered impolite or a little abrupt to just say, for example:

I don't want to do that.

or

I can't do that.

CONVERSATION PRACTICE WITH A FRIEND

1. Find a partner and practice these two conversations aloud.
2. Switch roles for extra practice.

Person A:	I have to decide between two jobs. One job is exciting, but the salary is terrible. The other job is boring, but the salary is fantastic. I don't know which one I should take.
Person B:	You should take the more exciting job. If you take the boring one, you'll be miserable.
Person A:	You're right. Thanks a lot, Dad.

Person A:	I'm really bored with school. The classes aren't interesting. I don't feel like I'm learning anything. What should I do?
Person B:	If you feel that way, you ought to quit school and find a job that you like.
Person A:	I can't do that because without a college degree good jobs are very hard to find.

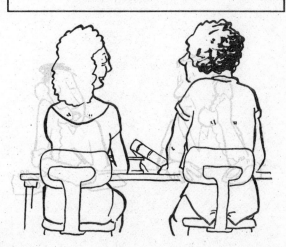

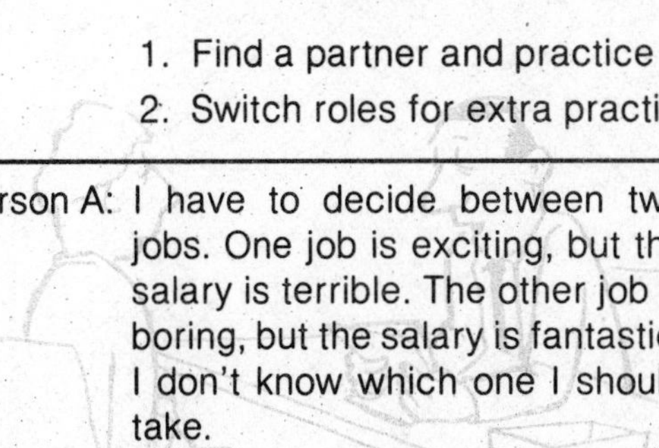

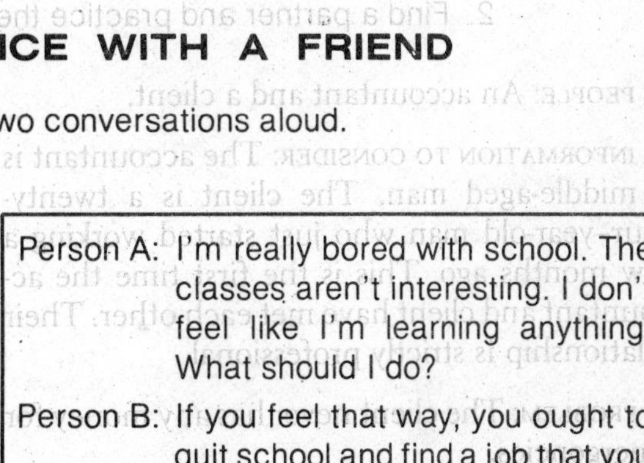

PEOPLE: A father and a son.

INFORMATION TO CONSIDER: The son is in his late twenties. He doesn't live at home; however, he still has a very close relationship with his father.

PROBLEM: The son has to choose between two jobs. One job is exciting with a low salary; the other job is boring with an excellent salary.

ADVICE: The father advises his son to take the exciting job because he knows his son would be miserable working in a boring job regardless of the money. The son thinks this is good advice.

PEOPLE: Two classmates.

INFORMATION TO CONSIDER: One student is a man; the other is a woman. They are both twenty-one years old. This is the first time they have taken a class together. They have a friendly relationship in the class, but they don't know each other very well. They never socialize outside of class.

PROBLEM: One of the classmates is very bored with his classes. He doesn't feel like he's learning anything.

ADVICE: The other classmate advises him to quit school and try to find a job he likes. He doesn't think that's such a good idea because without a college degree good jobs are hard to find.

Now You Try It

1. Read the following situations.
2. Find a partner and practice the conversations together.

PEOPLE: An accountant and a client.

INFORMATION TO CONSIDER: The accountant is a middle-aged man. The client is a twenty-four–year-old man who just started working a few months ago. This is the first time the accountant and client have met each other. Their relationship is strictly professional.

PROBLEM: The client never has any money for emergencies.

ADVICE: The accountant advises him to open a savings account into which he must deposit money every month. The client agrees with him.

PEOPLE: Two brothers.

INFORMATION TO CONSIDER: The two brothers are middle-aged. They live in different cities, but they still have a very close relationship.

PROBLEM: One brother is working two jobs. He is very tired and doesn't have enough time to spend with his family.

ADVICE: The other brother advises him to quit one of the jobs before he gets sick and can't work at all. The first brother says he can't do that because he has a lot of bills to pay right now.

PEOPLE: A travel agent and a customer.

INFORMATION TO CONSIDER: The travel agent is a woman in her late fifties. The customer is a man in his early thirties. This is the first time they have met. Their relationship is purely professional.

PROBLEM: The customer wants to take a trip to Paris, but he is afraid of flying.

ADVICE: The travel agent advises him to take a cruise on a ship. The customer thinks that is a wonderful idea.

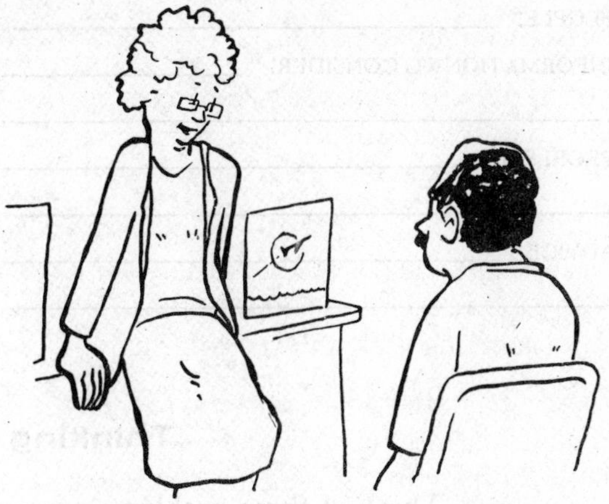

PEOPLE: Two good friends.

INFORMATION TO CONSIDER: Both friends are women in their late twenties. They have been good friends for several years and have a close relationship.

PROBLEM: One woman wants to buy a new stereo system, but she doesn't have enough money right now.

ADVICE: Her friend advises her to charge the stereo on a credit card and then pay for it in small monthly payments. The other woman says she won't do that because she doesn't believe in buying things on credit.*

* *Buying on credit* means paying for something over a period of months or years after purchasing it.

PEOPLE: A salesperson at a sports store and a customer.

INFORMATION TO CONSIDER: The salesperson is a woman in her early thirties. She is an experienced camper. The customer is a young man in his late teens. This is the first time this young man has come to this sports store. He and the salesperson do not know each other.

PROBLEM: The young man is going camping for the first time and he doesn't know what equipment to take.

ADVICE: The salesperson advises him to take a backpack, a sleeping bag, and a good pair of hiking boots. The client thinks that's a good idea.

PEOPLE: ______________________

INFORMATION TO CONSIDER: ______________________

____

PROBLEM: ______________________

____

ADVICE: ______________________

____

Thinking on Your Feet

Think of three problems you are having right now. Briefly write about them here:

example

I have had a cold for two weeks. I can't get rid of it.

1. ______________________

____

2. ______________________

____

3. ______________________

____

directions:

Explain one of your problems to someone in the class. Have that person give you advice about how to solve your problem. You can either accept his or her advice or turn it down. Continue until everyone has had a chance to discuss at least one problem.

Rotation Activity

Each person in this section has a problem and would like some advice. Read each situation and then offer advice to help him or her solve the problem. Write your advice in the spaces provided after each situation.

1. Sarah Brown is forty-seven years old. She is five feet, six inches tall and weighs 185 pounds. She desperately wants to lose weight. She has tried many different "fad" diets but none of them helped her. What should she do to lose weight?

____

____

____

2. Alan Watson is fifty-six years old. He has smoked cigarettes for thirty-five years. He wants to quit smoking but can't. He has tried to stop five times but always begins smoking again when he is angry or nervous. What should he do to quit smoking?

____

____

____

3. Isao Mitsui is a Japanese student studying English in the United States. He has been in the U.S. for one year. He studies very hard but feels his English isn't improving very quickly. He particularly wants to improve his listening and speaking skills. What should he do?

____

____

____

4. Sergio Gonzalez is studying business at a university in the U.S. He is very homesick. He wants to go home but knows he should continue his courses at the university. He misses his family so much that he can't concentrate on his studies and his grades are beginning to drop. What should he do to get rid of his homesickness?

____

____

____

5. Susan Black is twenty-three years old. She lives alone in a big city. Susan has two jobs and is taking one course at a community college. Lately Susan has noticed that she is often very nervous. Even if she sleeps a lot, she always feels very tired. Susan is afraid she will soon become very sick if she doesn't relax. What should she do?

____

____

____

6. Tim Campbell is thirty-one years old. He has drunk alcohol since he was sixteen years old. Lately he thinks he has been drinking too much at parties, at home, and alone. He wants to stop but finds it very difficult to do because his wife and all his friends like to drink. What should he do?

____

____

directions:

1. After offering your advice to these six people, find a partner.
2. Together choose one of the six preceding situations around which you can create a short role play.
3. One person has the problem; the other person is a counselor offering advice.
4. Practice your role play. When you feel comfortable with it, present it to your teachers or other people in the class.
5. Repeat steps one thru four with a new partner.

Stating Your Intention to Do Something

People state their intention to do something when they plan to act in a certain way. All the expressions in this section can be used in formal and informal situations.

You can state your intention by saying:

I am determined to . . .	strong	go on a diet.
I've decided to . . .	↑	quit smoking.
I'm going to . . .		look for a new job.
I intend to. . .	↓	go to a psychiatrist.
I'm planning to . . .	neutral	

To express approval or happiness about someone's intention, you can say:

	Excellent.	strong
	Wonderful.	↑
(That's)	Great.	
	Fine.	
	Nice.	
	Good.	
	All right.	↓
	OK.	neutral

To show surprise about someone's intention, you can say:

I'm surprised!
Really?
You're kidding!
Oh?

To express sorrow about someone's intention, you can say:

That's awful.	That's too bad.
That's terrible.	I'm sorry to hear that.
What a shame/pity.	I'm sorry.

The *strength* or *neutrality* of an expression showing surprise or expressing sorrow depends on the speaker's intonation. Ask your teacher to give you some examples.

You can state your intention by saying:

I am determined to . . .	↑ strong	go on a diet.
I've decided to . . .		quit smoking.
I'm going to . . .		look for a new job.
I intend to . . .		go to a psychiatrist.
I plan to . . .	↓ neutral	

If you want to express reservation about a person's intention to do something, you can say:

Have you considered that . . .	you might get sick.
Keep in mind that . . .	it might cost too much money.
One drawback is that . . .	you could eventually become very unhappy.
I'm worried that . . .	
That's a good idea, but . . .	you might not like moving to a new city.
A problem with that is . . .	

FOR A BETTER UNDERSTANDING

When expressing a reservation about someone's intention, you are indirectly showing concern that there might be a problem. For example:

I'm worried that . . .
A problem with that is . . .   you might not like living in an apartment.
One drawback is that . . .

Remember that the person to whom you are speaking has not asked for your opinion. So, generally speaking, it is a good idea to express your concern as a polite reservation: "Have you considered that you might not like living in an apartment?" rather than as a piece of advice: "You shouldn't move because you might not like living in an apartment."

CONVERSATION PRACTICE WITH A FRIEND

1. Find a partner and practice these conversations aloud.
2. Switch roles for extra practice.

Person A: I've decided to get a divorce.
Person B: What a shame. I didn't know that you and your wife were having problems.

Person A: I'm planning to buy a condominium next year because it's more convenient.
Person B: That's great, but a condominium might be very expensive to buy and maintain.

PEOPLE: Two coworkers.

INFORMATION TO CONSIDER: Both workers are middle-aged men. They have worked together for several years. They have a friendly but professional relationship. They don't do things together socially.

INTENTION: One of the men has decided to get a divorce. The other man is sorry about the situation. He didn't know that the first man and his wife were having problems.

PEOPLE: Two next-door neighbors.

INFORMATION TO CONSIDER: Both neighbors are in their late sixties. One is a woman; the other is a man. They live in houses next to each other. They have known each other for many years, and they are good friends.

INTENTION: The woman is planning to buy a condominium next year. The man expresses a reservation. He says that's a good idea but that condominiums can be very expensive to buy and maintain.

Now You Try It

1. Read the following situations.
2. Find a partner and practice the conversations together.

PEOPLE: Two roommates.

INFORMATION TO CONSIDER: Both roommates are twenty-three–year-old women. They have shared an apartment for two years and are very good friends.

INTENTION: One roommate is going to start jogging in order to lose weight. The other roommate is very surprised. She thought the first woman hated to exercise.

PEOPLE: A mother and a daughter.

INFORMATION TO CONSIDER: The daughter is thirty years old. She doesn't live with her mother. The mother and daughter have a very close, loving relationship.

INTENTION: The daughter is determined to go back to school this fall and get a bachelor's degree. Her mother expresses a reservation. One drawback is that her daughter will have to quit her job in order to go back to school.

PEOPLE: Two friends.

INFORMATION TO CONSIDER: Both friends are men in their late fifties. They are both farmers. They have lived near each other all of their lives and have a very close relationship.

INTENTION: One man has decided to sell his farm because it is too expensive to maintain. The other man is sorry about the decision because he is going to miss the first man.

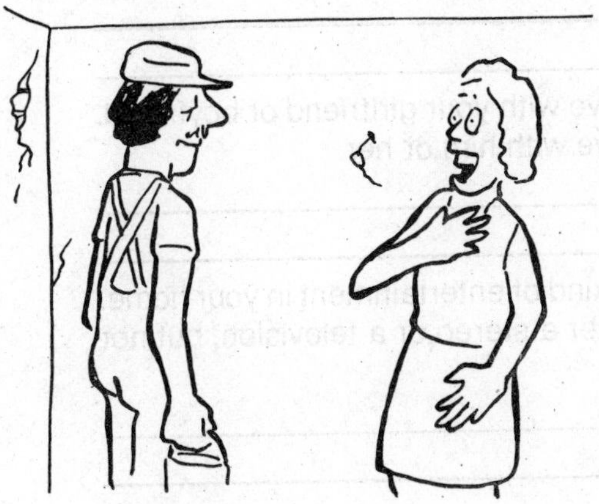

PEOPLE: A husband and a wife.

INFORMATION TO CONSIDER: Both people are in their late twenties. They have been married two years and have a loving relationship.

INTENTION: The husband is going to paint the living room because it looks terrible. At first the wife is surprised. Then she expresses her happiness about his decision.

PEOPLE: A boss and an employee.

INFORMATION TO CONSIDER: The boss is a middle-aged man. The employee is a woman in her early thirties. They have known each other for several years. They have a friendly but professional relationship.

INTENTION: The boss is planning to take a vacation next month. He has decided to put this employee in charge because she is very dependable. She is very surprised and thanks him for this opportunity.

PEOPLE: ______________________________

____

INFORMATION TO CONSIDER: ____________

____

____

INTENTION: ___________________________

____

____

Discussion Activity

1. Find a partner and read the following situations.
2. For each situation, decide which choice you are going to make.
3. Tell your partner how you plan to act and explain why.
4. Have your partner give his or her reaction by expressing:
   A. Approval
   B. Surprise
   C. Sorrow
   D. A reservation

1. *Situation:* Your company is giving you a two-week vacation.
   Choice: You can go to a tropical island or a snowy mountain.
   Decision: ______________________
   Reply: ______________________
2. *Situation:* You are very much in love with your girlfriend or boyfriend.
   Choice: You can get married or live with him or her.
   Decision: ______________________
   Reply: ______________________
3. *Situation:* You want to have some kind of entertainment in your home.
   Choice: You can afford to buy either a stereo or a television, but not both.
   Decision: ______________________
   Reply: ______________________
4. *Situation:* It is Friday evening.
   Choice: You can go to one of your friends' parties or you can stay at home and read a good book.
   Decision: ______________________
   Reply: ______________________
5. *Situation:* A good friend is wearing a shirt that looks silly on him or her. The friend just asked you how the shirt looks.
   Choice: You can lie and tell him or her it looks good. Or, you can tell your friend the truth and probably hurt his or her feelings.
   Decision: ______________________
   Reply: ______________________
6. *Situation:* You have a chance to take a trip across North America.
   Choice: You can go by car, by train, or by bus.
   Decision: ______________________
   Reply: ______________________
7. *Situation:* A friend is going to teach you a new sport.
   Choice: You can learn how to play golf or table tennis.
   Decision: ______________________
   Reply: ______________________
8. *Situation:* You have a serious personal problem.
   Choice: You can go to a psychiatrist or talk to a close friend.
   Decision: ______________________
   Reply: ______________________

9. *Situation:* You just won $1000 in a contest.
   Choice: You can spend it or put it in a savings account.
   Decision: ______________________________
   Reply: ______________________________
10. *Situation:* You have a very sick pet.
   Choice: You can let it die naturally or you can put it to sleep.*
   Decision: ______________________________
   Reply: ______________________________

* *To put a pet to sleep* means to kill an animal by giving it an overdose of an anesthetic.

One-Liners

1. Find a partner and choose one of the conversation lines.
2. Together create a conversation around that line.
3. Present your role play to the group.

conversation 1

LINE: "I'm determined to quit smoking."

PEOPLE: Two close friends.

SITUATION: The two friends are sitting in a restaurant having lunch. One friend just found out that he or she must quit smoking for health reasons.

conversation 2

LINE: "I've decided to give you one more chance."

PEOPLE: A boss and an employee.

SITUATION: The boss is very angry at the employee because of a big mistake he or she made. The boss wanted to fire the employee but has decided to give him or her one more chance.

conversation 3

LINE: "I'm going to adopt a baby."

PEOPLE: Two cousins who are very close.

SITUATION: They are in one of the cousins' living room. One of the cousins is going to adopt a baby because she and her husband can't have one of their own.

conversation 4

LINE: "I've decided to dye my hair bright red."

PEOPLE: A husband and a wife.

SITUATION: The couple is sitting at the kitchen table. The wife says that she has decided to dye her hair bright red. Her husband is shocked and unhappy.

conversation 5

LINE: "I'm planning to break out of jail tonight."

PEOPLE: Two convicts.

SITUATION: Both convicts are in their prison cell. One of the convicts desperately wants to break out of jail to see his or her family.

conversation 6

LINE: "I'm going to buy a new washing machine tomorrow."

PEOPLE: Two good friends.

SITUATION: One friend is visiting the other while he or she is doing the laundry. The washing machine just broke. Soap and water are spilling everywhere. This is the second time this month the machine has broken. The woman doing the laundry is very upset and says that she is definitely going to buy a new washing machine tomorrow.

COMMUNITY EXERCISES

This week ask the people listed in the following chart for some advice about a decision you have to make. Write the important information from your conversation in the chart on the following page. To ask for advice, you can say:

	What should I do?	
	What do you recommend?	
(I need some advice.)	or	quit school?
	Should I . . .	buy a used car or a new one?
	Do you think I should . . .	move to another apartment?

	What decision were you asking about?	*How did you ask for advice?*	*What reply did the other person give?*	*Was the situation formal or informal?*
Your teacher				
A classmate				
A neighbor				
A coworker				
A salesperson				

Watch T.V. for at least an hour. Try to find examples of people talking about specific plans (intentions) they have for the near future. How do the people express their intentions? How do the other people react? The best kinds of programs to watch are situational comedies or dramas, movies, or soap operas. Some television commercials might also have examples. Ask your teacher if you have any questions about whether a specific program would be useful.

	one	*two*
What was the title of the T.V. program? What type of program was it?	______ ______	______ ______
What types of people were involved in the scene in which someone stated his or her intention?	______ ______	______ ______
Was it a formal or an informal situation?	______	______
How did the person express his or her intention?	______ ______	______ ______
How did the other person react? Did he or she express happiness, surprise, sorrow, a reservation?	______ ______	______ ______
What expression did the other person use when responding?	______ ______	______ ______

PUTTING IT TOGETHER

If you've learned this chapter well, you should be able to: (1) advise someone about a particular decision, (2) accept or turn down someone else's advice; (3) state your intention to do something; (4) express happiness, surprise, sorrow, or a reservation about someone else's intention to do something.

What Would You Say?

1. A good friend calls you on the telephone and frantically tells you that his eight-year-old son hasn't come home from school yet, and it's 7:30 P.M. You advise him by saying:

   ____

2. Your husband or wife comes home and tells you that he or she has decided to quit working. You are very surprised. So, you reply by saying:

   ____

3. A little girl who lives next door apologizes for breaking your window. She was playing baseball and accidentally hit the ball through the glass. You accept her apology by saying:

____

4. A coworker got a big promotion at work. You are very happy for him. You walk into his office and congratulate him by saying:

____

5. You are a university academic advisor. One of your students failed four of his five courses last semester. You advise him about the next semester by saying:

____

6. It is the first day of classes. You sit down next to a person you don't know. You turn to her and introduce yourself by saying:

____

7. A close friend has invited you to her house for dinner tomorrow night. You aren't sure yet if you can go. So, you reply by saying:

____

8. Your brother failed his final history exam this semester. When you find out, you offer your condolences to him by saying:

____

9. One of your classmates told you that her wallet with her driver's license and credit cards was stolen last night. You advise her by saying:

____

10. You are talking to a professor when you notice that you are late for your next class. You say to her:

____

11. You want to borrow your roommate's tape recorder. You ask his permission by saying:

____

12. Your next-door neighbor is having a lot of trouble starting his car this morning. You offer to help by saying:

____

13. Your roommate just told you that she is planning to buy a dog. You state your reservation to her intentions by saying:

____

14. You are studying for a big exam. Your next-door neighbors are being very noisy. You ask them not to make so much noise by saying:

____

15. You are at the train station. You are saying goodbye to a close friend. You won't see the friend for a long time. You tell him goodbye by saying:

____

16. Your coworker tells you that she has had a very bad toothache for the last two days. You advise her by saying:

____

17. It is Monday morning. You see your boss as you walk in the front door. You greet him by saying:

____

18. A good friend just told you that he really likes your new haircut. You reply by saying:

____

19. A classmate just asked you to help him study for an exam. You turn him down by saying:

____

20. A close neighbor tells you that he received a bill for a set of encyclopedias that he never bought. You advise him by saying:

____

Build-Up Role Plays

Create your own role play as a class (or in small groups if the class is large). Use the following directions. Then repeat the build-up process to create other role plays.

FIRST PERSON: Choose the functions which you want to use in the role play. Select them from this list:

Introducing Others or Yourself	Requests
Greetings	Warnings, Commands, Directions
Small-Talk Topics	Conversation Closings and Goodbyes
Invitations	Offering to Do Something
Apologies	Seeking Permission
Condolences	Advising Someone
Expressions of Gratitude	Stating Your Intention to Do Something
Compliments, Congratulations	

SECOND PERSON: Give a setting for the role play.

THIRD PERSON: Create a role-play situation in that setting, including the players.

FOURTH PERSON: Name the important details to consider to make the role play realistic, including information about the players.

FIFTH, SIXTH, SEVENTH . . . (AS MANY AS NECESSARY) PERSON: Act out the role play.

Sticky Situations

Discuss these situations together.

1. An acquaintance constantly gives you advice which you don't want or don't ask for. What should you do?
2. You expressed a reservation about a person's intention to do something. Now that person is very upset with you. What should you do?

CHAPTER 9

PLEASURE
DISPLEASURE

- Expressing Pleasure
- Expressing Displeasure

Expressing Pleasure

People express that they like (doing) something when they feel an attraction for (doing) that thing. Some commonly used expressions in English are:

	formal ↑ informal ↓	
I'm (really) fond of * . . .		the funny stories my father tells me.
I (really) enjoy . . .		eating Mexican food.
I (really) like . . .		kittens and puppies.
I (really) love . . .		watching war movies.

You can agree by saying:

I do too./I am too.*
So do I./So am I.*
Me too.

You can disagree by saying:

(Oh?) (Really?) I don't./I'm not.**
Not me.

*To agree with the expression *I'm fond of*, you say: *I am too*, or *So am I*, or *Me too*.

**To disagree with the expression *I'm fond of*, you say: *I'm not*, or *Not me*.

FOR A BETTER UNDERSTANDING

It is important to point out that the just-listed expressions convey different *degrees* of pleasure. Look at the following scale:

I'm fond of . . . ↑	Weak degree of pleasure
I enjoy . . .	
I like . . .	
I love . . . ↓	Strong degree of pleasure

Generally speaking, *the more informal* the expression, *the stronger* the degree of pleasure it implies.

Look at the following pairs of statements. Decide in each pair which statement conveys the strongest degree of pleasure.

1. I really love eating hamburgers.
   I'm fond of hamburgers.
2. I enjoy eating chocolate ice cream.
   I love eating chocolate ice cream.
3. I like small cars.
   I really love small cars.
4. I'm fond of soccer.
   I really like soccer.

CONVERSATION PRACTICE WITH A FRIEND

1. Find a partner and practice these two conversations aloud.
2. Switch roles for extra practice.

Person A:	I love visiting New York City. There are so many restaurants, hotels, and museums to visit.
Person B:	I don't. New York City is too crowded and dirty.

PEOPLE: Two brothers.

INFORMATION TO CONSIDER: Both of the brothers are middle-aged. They live in the same city, but have their own homes. They often socialize together and have a close, friendly relationship.

LIKE: One brother likes to visit New York City whenever he can. He likes the many restaurants, hotels, and museums. The other brother disagrees. He thinks New York City is too crowded and dirty.

Person A:	I really like snow. It makes everything look so pretty.
Person B:	I do too. When it snows, I can go skiing and sledding.

PEOPLE: Two people who don't know each other.

INFORMATION TO CONSIDER: Both people are in their late teens. One is a young man; the other is a young woman. They are waiting for a bus at the bus stop. It is snowing.

LIKE: To make small talk, the young woman says that she really likes snow because everything looks pretty. The young man also likes snow because he can go skiing and sledding.

Now You Try It

1. Read the following situations.
2. Find a partner and practice the conversations together.

PEOPLE: Two English students.

INFORMATION TO CONSIDER: One student is a twenty-five–year-old man. The other is a middle-aged woman. They are taking the same English course together. They know each other well and have a friendly relationship.

LIKE: One student really likes American coffee. He drinks ten cups of coffee a day. The other student disagrees. She hates American coffee because it is too weak and tastes funny.

PEOPLE: Two acquaintances at a party.

INFORMATION TO CONSIDER: Both people at the party are men. They are in their late twenties. Both people are good friends with the hostess of the party but they don't know each other very well.

LIKE: One man is saying that he really likes to smoke marijuana at parties because it relaxes him. The other person disagrees. He likes having some drinks at a party.

PEOPLE: Two people on a date.

INFORMATION TO CONSIDER: The man is in his early thirties. The woman is in her late twenties. This is their first date. They don't know each other very well yet. They are at dinner now.

LIKE: The man says that he enjoys listening to jazz. The woman agrees. She likes jazz because it has so much variety.

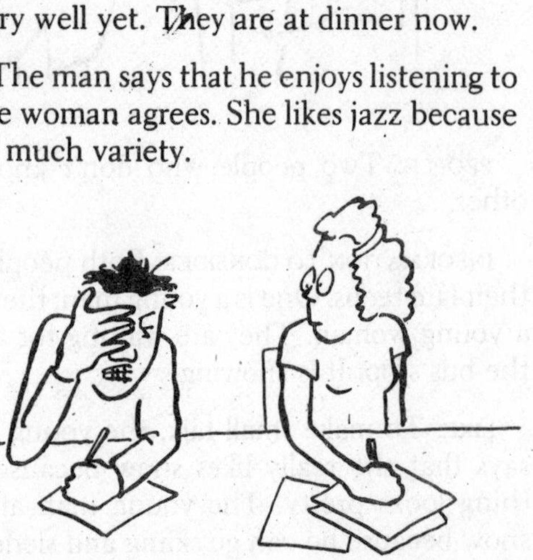

PEOPLE: Two friends.

INFORMATION TO CONSIDER: One friend is a twenty-year-old-man. The other is a twenty-year-old woman. They have known each other since childhood. They have a close, friendly relationship.

LIKE: One friend really likes writing letters to people. The other friend disagrees because it takes too much time.

PEOPLE: Two roommates.

INFORMATION TO CONSIDER: Both roommates are middle-aged women. They have been friends for a while. They are eating dinner. Both women have vacations coming up in the near future.

LIKE: One woman says that she likes to travel to new cities during her vacations. The other woman disagrees. She likes to stay home and rest during her vacations.

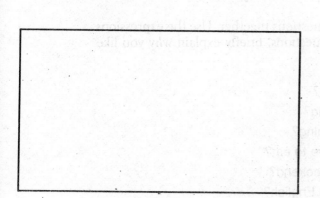

PEOPLE: ____________________

____

INFORMATION TO CONSIDER: ____________________

____

____

____

LIKE: ____________________

____

____

Rotation Role Play

people	*what do you like about . . .*
1. An immigration officer	1. Your English-language school?
2. A classmate	2. Your apartment/home?
3. A local newspaper reporter	3. North American television?*
4. A stranger	4. North American food?*
5. A teacher	5. The U.S. political system?*
6. A parent	6. North American grocery stores?*
7. A bartender at your favorite bar	7. North American cars?*
8. ____________________	8. ____________________

* If you are not studying English in North America, answer these questions about the country in which you are living.

Imagine that you feel:

• Excited	• Hesitant
• Shocked	• Pleased
• Extremely happy	• Surprised
• Astonished	• Uninterested

directions:

1. Find a partner. Suppose one of you is an English student. Have the other be one of the just-listed people.
2. Have that person ask the student several of the just-listed questions, which the student should answer.
3. The other person can either agree or disagree using one of the emotions listed. (Try to identify the emotion your partner is feeling.)
4. Repeat steps one to four several times with different partners.

Discussion Activity

Find a partner and discuss these questions together. Use the expressions on page 166. When discussing the questions, briefly explain *why* you like something.

1. What kind of movies do you like?
2. What sports do you enjoy playing?
3. What sports do you enjoy watching?
4. What is one kind of food you love to eat?
5. What do you like to do on the weekend?
6. What do you like about studying English?
7. What do you enjoy doing on vacation?
8. What kind of music are you fond of?
9. What kind of music do you really love?
10. What kind of weather do you like?
11. What do you enjoy buying for yourself when you have some extra money?
12. What kind of pets are you fond of?
13. What kind of parties do you enjoy? Big? Small? Noisy? Quiet? Intimate?
14. ______________________________

Expressing Displeasure

People express that they dislike (doing) something when they feel displeased about (doing) that thing. Some commonly used expressions are:

I'm not fond of . . .	↑ formal	taking care of these noisy children.
I don't (particularly) care for . . .		this salad dressing.
I don't enjoy . . .		drinking coffee for breakfast.
I don't like . . .		disco music.
I can't stand . . .	informal ↓	studying late at night.

You can agree by saying:

I don't either./I'm not either.*/I can't either.†
Neither do I./Neither am I.*/Neither can I.†
Me neither.

* To agree with the expression *I'm not fond of,* you say: *I'm not either,* or *Neither am I,* or *Me neither.*
† To agree with the expression *I can't stand,* you say: *I can't either,* or *Neither can I,* or *Me neither.*

You can disagree by saying:

(Oh?) (Really?) I do./I am.**

** To disagree with the expression *I'm not fond of,* you say: *I am.*

To disagree with the expression *I can't stand,* you can say: *Really? I like . . .*

You can also express your dislike of (doing) something by saying:

I dislike . . .	(quite formal)	horror movies.
I hate . . .	(informal)	going to work.
		getting up.

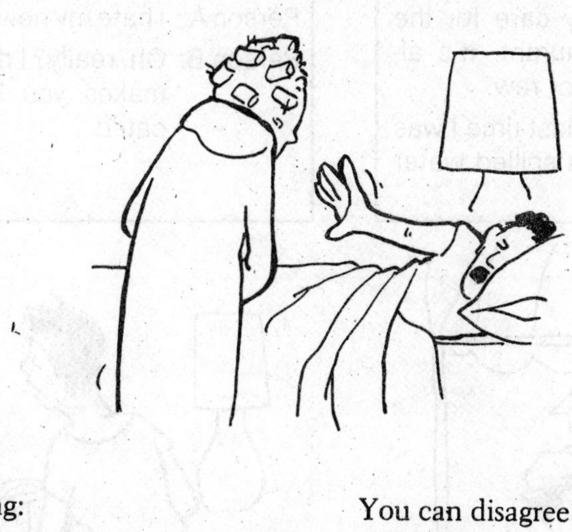

You can agree by saying:

I do too.
So do I.
Me too.

You can disagree by saying:

I don't.
Not me.

FOR A BETTER UNDERSTANDING

The expressions on pages 170 and 171 convey different degrees of displeasure. Look at the following scale:

I'm not fond of . . .	↑ weak degree of displeasure
I don't (particularly) care for . . .	
I dislike . . .	
I don't enjoy . . .	
I don't like . . .	
I can't stand . . .	
I hate . . .	↓ strong degree of displeasure

Generally speaking, *the more informal* the expression, *the stronger* the degree of displeasure it implies.

Look at the following pairs of statements. Decide in each pair which statement conveys the strongest degree of displeasure.

1. I'm not fond of hot weather.
   I can't stand hot weather.
2. I hate television.
   I don't particularly care for television.
3. I don't like classical music.
   I'm not fond of classical music.
4. I don't enjoy big parties.
   I really hate big parties.

CONVERSATION PRACTICE WITH A FRIEND

1. Find a partner and practice these two conversations aloud.
2. Switch roles for extra practice.

Person A: I don't particularly care for the food in that restaurant. It's always overcooked or raw.

Person B: I don't either. The last time I was there the waitress spilled water on me.

Person A: I hate my new haircut!

Person B: Oh, really? I don't. I really like it. It makes you look more sophisticated.

PEOPLE: A computer sales representative and a client.

INFORMATION TO CONSIDER: The sales representative is a woman in her early thirties. The client is a man in his late fifties. They don't know each other very well. They occasionally get together to discuss business matters. Their relationship is strictly professional.

DISLIKE: The client and the representative are going to have lunch together. They are standing outside one restaurant. The client doesn't like this restaurant because the food is always overcooked or raw. The sales representative agrees. The last time she was there a waitress spilled water on her.

PEOPLE: Two sisters.

INFORMATION TO CONSIDER: Both sisters are teenagers and they live together at home. They have a very close relationship.

DISLIKE: One sister just had her hair cut very short. She is very upset and hates the haircut. The other sister disagrees with her. She likes her sister's haircut. She thinks it makes her look more sophisticated.

Now You Try It

1. Read the following situations.
2. Find a partner and practice the conversations together.

PEOPLE: Two next-door neighbors in an apartment building.

INFORMATION TO CONSIDER: Both people are women. One woman is twenty-one years old. The other is in her late fifties. They have known each other for a few years, but they don't have a close relationship. They only talk when they see each other in the hall.

DISLIKE: The two neighbors are talking together in the hall. During their conversation, the younger woman says that she doesn't like living in an apartment because there is no privacy and it's too crowded. The other woman disagrees. She likes living in an apartment because it is easy to take care of.

PEOPLE: Two strangers at a local laundromat.

INFORMATION TO CONSIDER: One person is a man; the other is a woman. They are both in their twenties. They have never met each other before.

DISLIKE: They are both doing their laundry at a neighborhood laundromat. The man tells the woman that he can't stand doing laundry. The woman strongly agrees. She especially hates doing laundry in a laundromat because it takes so much time and is very inconvenient.

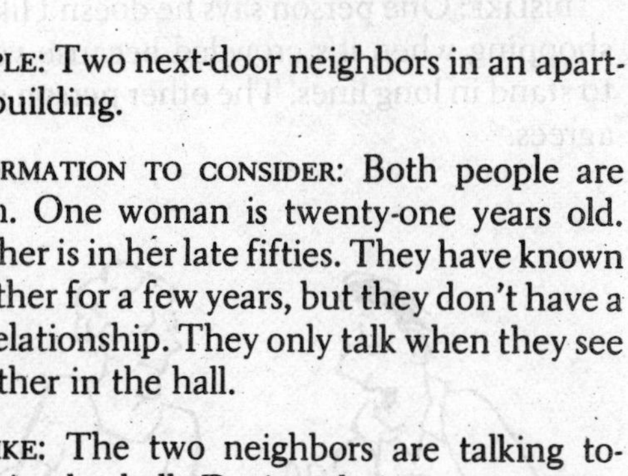

PEOPLE: Two good friends.

INFORMATION TO CONSIDER: Both friends are women in their early thirties. They have a very close relationship. Right now they are standing in front of a bakery shop window. Both women are on diets.

DISLIKE: One woman says she hates to diet. It's so boring. The other woman agrees. She dislikes dieting because she's hungry all the time.

PEOPLE: Two people who don't know each other.

INFORMATION TO CONSIDER: Two people who don't know each other are standing in a long line at a department store. They have been waiting a long time to pay for their purchases. Both people are men in their late fifties.

DISLIKE: One person says he doesn't like going shopping when it's crowded because you have to stand in long lines. The other person strongly agrees.

PEOPLE: Two classmates.

INFORMATION TO CONSIDER: Two classmates in college are having coffee together before their class begins. One classmate is a man; the other is a woman. They are in their twenties. They have become good friends during the semester.

DISLIKE: While they are drinking coffee, one classmate says that he hated high school. The other classmate disagrees. She said that she had a great time in high school and made a lot of friends there.

PEOPLE: ______________________

____

INFORMATION TO CONSIDER: ______________________

____

____

DISLIKE: ______________________

____

____

____

Thinking on Your Feet

Form a circle for this activity.

1. One person begins by telling the group one thing he or she doesn't like (doing), using one of the expressions on page 170 or 171.
2. The person sitting to the right disagrees and then tells the group one thing he or she doesn't like (doing). The next person then disagrees, and so on. Look at the following example.

   Person A: I don't enjoy eating sardines.
   Person B: Really? I do. I love eating sardines.

   Person B: I hate getting up early in the morning.
   Person C: Oh, really? I don't. I enjoy getting up early.

   Person C: I don't like country western music.
   Person D: Really? I do . . .
3. Continue around the circle in the same way.

One-Sided Dialogue

1. Read the following dialogue. Only Person A's lines are given.
2. Fill in the dialogue for Person B. Read Person A's lines carefully. They give you hints about what Person B is saying.
3. When you complete the dialogue, practice it with someone.

Two coworkers are having a discussion about where they live. Person A likes living in a big city. Person B likes living in the country.

A: You know, I really enjoy living in a big city.

B: ______________________________

____

A: But the noise, the people, and the tall buildings make a city exciting.

B: That's true, but______________________________

____

A: Me neither. I must admit I can't stand all the traffic. It causes too much pollution.

B: And I also hate______________________________

____

A: Yeah, so do I. The violence is terrible. But there's violence in small towns too, you know. Come on . . . isn't there anything you enjoy about big cities?

B: ______________________________

____

A: Me too. I try to go to a new movie or a play at least once a week. Why do you enjoy living in the country so much, anyway?

B. ______________________________

____

A: Really? Not me. I think it's *too* quiet in the country. And I don't like driving a long distance to get to a doctor's office or a grocery store.

B: Me neither but ______________________________

____

A: Yeah, so do I. I miss all the grass, trees, and flowers. They're hard to find in the city.

B: ______________________________

______________________________?

A: That sounds like fun. I'd love to spend the weekend out in the country. Thanks for asking. And maybe sometime soon you can spend a night with me in the city and we can go to a play or a movie.

Choose the Dialogue

1. Following are two conversations. Find a partner to help you practice one of them. Before you begin, cover up your partner's side of the dialogue.
2. Person A begins the conversation by reading 1. Person B chooses one of the replies in 2 and reads it to Person A.
3. Person A then reads the appropriate answer in 3. There is only one correct choice.
4. Continue the conversation. It's very important to listen to what your partner says.

person a	*person b*
1. I'm not enjoying this vacation at all.	*2.* Me neither. I hate camping in this park. The travel agency gave us terrible advice. or Really? I am. I love this cruise.
3. Well, I don't. The weather is terrible and I'm seasick. I want to get off at the next port and fly home. or That's for sure. It's too crowded here. I don't like all these people and trailers.	*4.* You're kidding! It's too early to leave. The cruise just started. Don't you like anything about the cruise? or Me neither. And look, there's garbage everywhere. The campers are destroying this park.
5. Well . . . I guess it isn't too bad. I must admit that I love the delicious seafood they are serving. or You're right. Let's leave right away. I can't stand it here.	*6.* I can't either. Let's pack the car and go home. or So do I. I really like the lobster and shrimp. Come on. Let's eat lunch. I'm hungry.

COMMUNITY EXERCISE

This week watch a talk show on the television. (You can ask your teacher for the names and times of some talk shows in your community.) Listen for examples of people saying they like or dislike things. People frequently state their pleasure or displeasure about things on this type of program. Write down the information you hear in the following chart.

	one	*two*	*three*
What was the title of the talk show?			
What person was talking on the program (a movie star, an author, a T.V. host)?			
Did the person say that he or she liked or disliked something?			
Write the statement here.			
Was the situaton formal or informal?			
Did you hear any new expressions for stating that you like or dislike something? Write them here.			

Think of six questions you would like to ask English speakers about what they like or don't like (doing). Write your questions here:

example

At what restaurants do you like to eat?

1. __________
2. __________
3. __________
4. __________
5. __________
6. __________

Interview at least two people. Write their answers here. Bring your information to class. Be prepared to discuss your findings with the others in the group.

one	***two***
1. ____________	1. ____________
2. ____________	2. ____________
3. ____________	3. ____________
4. ____________	4. ____________
5. ____________	5. ____________
6. ____________	6. ____________

PUTTING IT TOGETHER

If you've learned this chapter well, you should be able to (1) express your pleasure about (doing) something; (2) express your displeasure about (doing) something; and (3) agree or disagree with someone's pleasure or displeasure about (doing) something.

Supply an appropriate statement or response in each of the following spaces.

1. I love rock and roll music.	____________
2. ____________	Neither do I.
3. You really ought to take a vacation this summer and get some rest.	____________
4. ____________	No, thank you for asking, but I'm already busy tomorrow night.
5. Would you like me to help you fix dinner?	____________
6. Is it all right if I borrow your car tonight?	____________
7. ____________	Oh, really? I do. I love big dogs.
8. Will you please bring me a cup of tea?	____________
9. I'm sorry that I forgot my homework assignment, Mr. Jones.	____________
10. ____________	You're welcome.
11. Hi, Betty, How's it going?	____________
12. I was very sorry to hear that your aunt died.	____________
13. What a beautiful apartment!	____________
14. I hate thunderstorms.	____________
15. It's getting late. I have to go.	____________

16. ____________ Thanks for asking, but I've already finished.

17. My sister told me that you are getting married. Congratulations! ____________

18. ____________ Of course. I'd be glad to.

19. I don't particularly care for this kind of art. ____________

20. ____________ Nice to meet you, Karen.

Role Plays

directions:

1. Following are several role-play situations. Find a partner and together choose a role play that interests you.
2. Read the *Situation and Setting* sections carefully. Decide together which expressions, forms of address, and nonverbal body language are most appropriate for your roles.
3. Pay special attention to details and props. This makes your role play more realistic and fun. A list of details to consider is included in each role play.
4. Practice your conversation several times. When you feel comfortable with your conversation, present it to the class.
5. Before you begin, give some details of the players, their relationship to each other, and the situation and setting.

1. SITUATION AND SETTING: A couple is looking at a house they might buy. As they walk through the rooms they talk about what they like and don't like. When they are finished, they have a cup of coffee together and decide whether or not they want to buy the house.

PLAYERS: A young couple.

DETAILS TO CONSIDER

Your names

House setting to walk about in

A place to have a cup of coffee

Exactly what you like and don't like about the house and why

Nonverbal body language

2. SITUATION AND SETTING: Two friends are visiting a city for the first time. (Choose a city with which you are both familiar.) They are sitting in their hotel having a drink. They are talking about what they like and don't like about the city. They have too much to see in the one day they have left. So, together they decide which is the most important place to visit on their last day.

PLAYERS: Two friends.

DETAILS TO CONSIDER

Relationship of the two friends (close? distant?)	Exactly what you like and don't like about the city.
Your names	The place you decide to visit on the last day and why
Forms of address	Nonverbal body language
Hotel-room setting	

3. SITUATION AND SETTING: Two business partners are having an important meeting. They have to find a new office building for their growing company. They must choose between: (1) an old, historic building in the city; (2) a tall, modern building in the city; or (3) a short, modern building in the suburbs. At their meeting the two partners discuss what they like and dislike about each building. Then together they decide which building they think is best and why.

PLAYERS: Two business partners.

DETAILS TO CONSIDER

Your names	Exactly what you like and don't like about each building
Forms of address	The building you decide to buy and why
Office setting	Nonverbal body language
Type of company you have	

4. SITUATION AND SETTING: Two friends have gone to the zoo together to look at the animals. They stop at a bench in the park to have something to drink. The talk about animals they like and don't like. Then they have a discussion about whether or not it is good to have zoos and keep animals in cages. One friend enjoys going to zoos. The other does not particularly care for them.

PLAYERS: Two friends.

DETAILS TO CONSIDER

Relationship of the friends (close? distant?)	Which animals you like and don't like
Your names	Details of why you like or don't like zoos
Forms of address	Nonverbal body language
Park bench in a zoo setting	

Sticky Situations

Discuss these situations together.

1. You just met a new friend's little brother. Your friend asked you if you like his little brother. You don't, but you are afraid that if you say so, you will hurt your friend's feelings. What should you do?
2. You met a person and have been talking together for a few minutes. During your conversation, you say that you hate children. The person to whom you are talking tells you he has five children. What should you say to that person?

CHAPTER 10

EXPRESSING YOUR OPINION
ASKING PEOPLE TO REPEAT THEMSELVES
INTERRUPTING SOMEONE
CHANGING THE TOPIC OF CONVERSATION

- Expressing Your Opinion
- Asking People to Repeat Themselves
- Interrupting Someone
- Changing the Topic of Conversation

Expressing Your Opinion

People often express their opinions when having a conversation with someone. You express your opinion when you want to give your point of view about a particular matter. Some commonly used expressions in English are:

	formal ↕ informal	
I am of the opinion that . . .	formal	we should call the police.
As far as I'm concerned . . .		she made the right decision.
Speaking for myself . . .		we can finish the assignment on time.
In my opinion . . .		children today watch too much T.V.
I believe/think that . . .		he should go on a diet.
If you ask me . . .	informal	

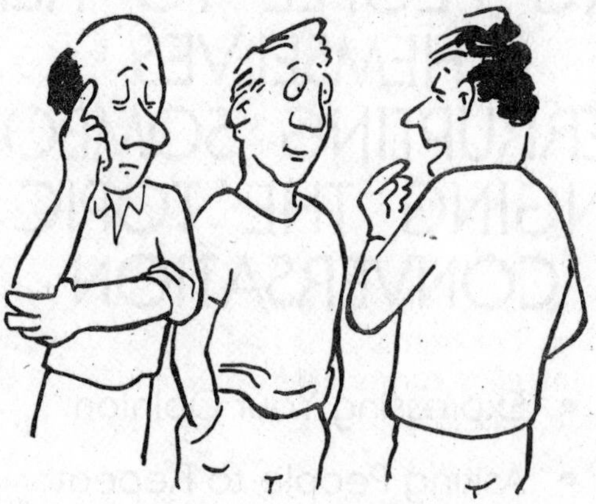

To agree with someone's opinion, you can say:

I couldn't agree with you more.	formal
I agree (with you entirely).	
You're (absolutely) right.	
(That's) true.	
(That's a) good point.	
I feel the same way.	
Of course.	
Right.	
I'll say.	
That's for sure.	informal

To show surprise about someone's opinion, you can say:

I'm surprised you feel that way.	formal
Oh?	
Really?	
You're kidding!	informal

To disagree with someone's opinion, you can say:

I can't possibly agree with you.	formal
I'm afraid I disagree with you.	
I disagree with you because . . .	
On the other hand . . .	
Well, in my opinion . . .	
Yes, but . . .	
I don't agree.	
You're wrong.	informal

FOR A BETTER UNDERSTANDING

When *agreeing with*, *disagreeing with*, or *showing surprise about* someone's opinion, it is a good idea to explain why you feel that way. By doing this, you give the other person an opportunity to make additional comments and keep the conversation going. For example:

Person A: In my opinion, children watch too much T.V.

Person B: I don't agree. Television keeps them entertained. So, they don't get bored and cause trouble.

Person A: Yes, but children are too inactive when they watch T.V. They just look at other people doing things.

Person B: I disagree with you because . . .

In this conversation, the speakers are always disagreeing with each other. In an actual conversation, however, there is usually a mixture of reactions to someone's opinions. For example, at first you might agree with the other person, then you might be surprised at what he or she says, and a little later in the conversation, you might disagree with an opinion. It is this variety that makes conversations interesting.

Look at the expressions used to show surprise on page 182. Generally speaking, *the more informal* the expression, *the stronger* the degree of surprise it implies. However, the strength or neutrality of these expressions to show surprise often depends on your intonation. Ask your teacher to demonstrate how these two conversations differ in their degree of surprise.

Person A: I'm going to finish this chapter in a few minutes.

Person B: Really? Then we'll still have time to go to the movies.

Person A: I'm going to get married this weekend.

Person B: Really?!? Why didn't you tell me sooner?

CONVERSATION PRACTICE WITH A FRIEND

1. Find a partner and practice these two conversations aloud.
2. Switch roles for extra practice.

Person A:	I think you should call your doctor. You're very sick and need some medicine.
Person B:	You're right. I'm going to call my doctor right now for an appointment.

Person A:	In my opinion, we need to hire ten new employees immediately.
Person B:	I'm afraid I disagree. I think we should give our current employees a raise* and ask them to do more work.

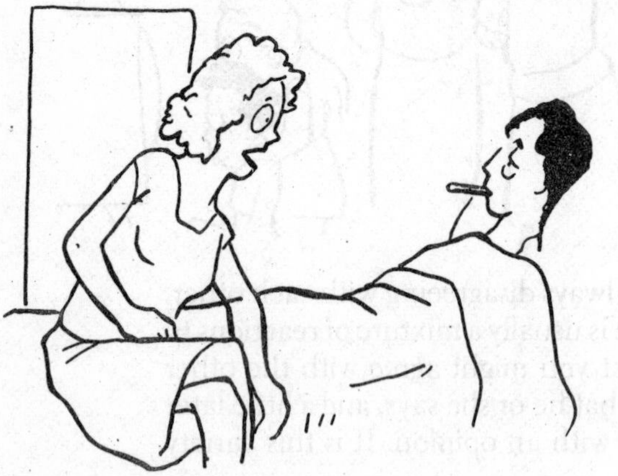

PEOPLE: Two good friends.

INFORMATION TO CONSIDER: Both people are women in their early thirties. They have known each other for many years and have a close relationship.

OPINION: One of the women is very sick. Her friend is visiting her and says that she should go to the doctor. The sick woman agrees and decides to call her doctor right now.

PEOPLE: Two business executives.

INFORMATION TO CONSIDER: One person is a man; the other is a woman. They are both middle-aged. Both people are business executives for a large company. They rarely work together in the company and don't know each other very well. Their relationship is strictly professional.

OPINION: The company needs some extra work done. These two people are trying to decide how to do it. One of them believes that the company needs to hire ten new employees immediately. The other executive disagrees. He believes the company should give the current employees a raise* and ask them to do more work.

* A *raise* is an increase in salary.

Now You Try It

1. Read the following situations.
2. Find a partner and practice the conversations together.

PEOPLE: Two politicians.

INFORMATION TO CONSIDER: One politician is a man in his early thirties. The other is a woman in her late fifties. They both want to be the mayor* of their city. They know each other but are not really friendly with each other. Their relationship is strictly professional.

OPINION: The two politicians are having a debate about the construction of a city sports center. One of the politicians believes that building the sports center is a good idea because children need a place to play. The other politician disagrees because it would cost the city too much money.

*The *mayor* is the elected leader of a city or town.

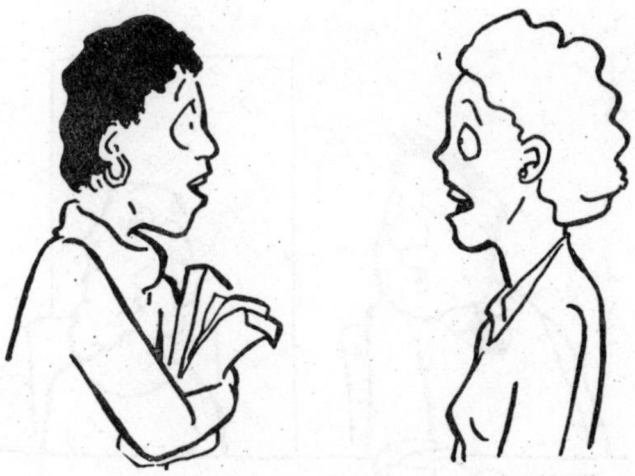

PEOPLE: Two students.

INFORMATION TO CONSIDER: Both students are seventeen-year-old women. They are in the same English class. They have known each other for several months and have a close, friendly relationship.

OPINION: One woman thinks that the English course is not very interesting. The other woman is surprised because she thought the first woman really liked the English course.

PEOPLE: Two coworkers.

INFORMATION TO CONSIDER: Both workers are middle-aged men. They have worked together for many years at the same construction company. They are good friends and often socialize together.

OPINION: The two friends are eating lunch together. One friend says that, in his opinion, income taxes are too high. His friend agrees. He believes that the average person has to proportionately pay more money than rich people.

PEOPLE: A man and a woman.

INFORMATION TO CONSIDER: The man is middle-aged. The woman is in her early twenties. They are at the party of a mutual friend and have never met each other before.

OPINION: The two people have been talking together for a while. They just started talking about the Equal Rights Movement.* The man says that, in his opinion, women should work at home and raise a family. The woman strongly disagrees. She believes that women should have the choice to work inside or outside of the home depending on their interests or needs.

* The *Equal Rights Movement* promotes equal privileges and responsibilities for both men and women.

PEOPLE: A father and a daughter.

INFORMATION TO CONSIDER: The father is in his late forties. The daughter is sixteen years old. She still lives at home and has a close relationship with her father.

OPINION: The father and daughter are talking together about drugs at the dinner table. The father says he believes that marijuana should be legalized because the government could then control its use. His daughter is very surprised at his opinion. She thought her father opposed legalizing marijuana because it was harmful.

PEOPLE: ____________________

____

INFORMATION TO CONSIDER: ____________________

____

____

OPINION: ____________________

____

____

____

Rotation Activity

directions:

1. Here is a list of people and the crimes they committed. Pick a person and give your opinion how to punish each criminal (if at all).
2. Show your opinion to another person. That person can either agree with, disagree with, or show surprise about your opinion and explain why. Discuss your opinions.
3. When you finish your discussion, repeat steps 1 and 2 with someone else.

person	*crime*
A young child	shoplifted a candy bar.
A sixteen-year-old boy	hurt an old lady.
An exconvict	*murdered a person.*
An executive businessperson	robbed $1 million from a bank using a computer.
A sixteen-year-old girl	vandalized a car.
An unemployed middle-aged man	forged a check for money to buy groceries for his hungry family.

A young child — shoplifted a candy bar.
Opinion: ____________________

A sixteen-year-old boy — hurt an old lady.
Opinion: ____________________

An exconvict — *murdered a person.*
Opinion: ____________________

An executive businessperson — robbed $1 million from a bank using a computer.
Opinion: ____________________

A sixteen-year-old girl — vandalized a car.
Opinion: ____________________

An unemployed middle-aged man — forged a check for money to buy groceries for his hungry family.
Opinion: ____________________

Problem-Solving Activity

directions:

1. Following are three problems that three communities must solve. Divide into groups of five people each.
2. As a group, choose one of the problems that interests you.

3. Become one of the five people in the community and together try to find a solution to your community's problem.
4. To begin, someone in the group gives his or her opinion. Another person can agree with, disagree with, or show surprise about the opinion and explain why.
5. Keep discussing until you find a solution to the problem. Remember that you must express the opinions of the person you are playing.

problems	*people in the community*
1. Your community has the opportunity to build a factory that manufactures weapons and ammunition. It would be helpful because the factory would create new jobs and produce money for the community. However, some people are opposed to the production and storage of weapons so close to homes and businesses.	• The mayor of the community • An unemployed citizen • The businessperson who wants to build the factory • The president of a club which supports gun control • A citizen once badly hurt in a gun accident
2. The state government wants to build a prison in your community. Knowing this would probably be an unpopular request, the government is also offering your community $10,000 a year, which it desperately needs. Some people think it's a good idea to build the prison in order to get the extra money. Others think it is unsafe and will create too many problems for the residents.	• The mayor of the community • The government official in charge of the state penal system • A citizen who would live near the prison • A citizen who has two small children • A police officer
3. Your community has a lot of trash that is not only ugly, but dangerous to the citizens' health. The community wants to find a way to get rid of the trash and keep the city clean. The citizens have different ideas about how to solve the problem.	• The mayor of the community • A citizen who believes that trash is the city government's problem • A citizen who believes that it is the individual's problem • The owner of the local trash-disposal company • A citizen with two small children

Asking People to Repeat Themselves

When having a conversation, you often need to ask someone to repeat what he or she just said. Maybe you didn't hear what the other person said or maybe you didn't understand properly. Some of the commonly used expressions are:

I beg your pardon?	formal ↑
Would you mind repeating that?	
Could you repeat that?	
Could you say that again?	
Pardon me?	
Excuse me?	
(I'm sorry) I didn't hear you.	
(I'm sorry) I didn't catch/get that.	
Sorry?	
What?	informal ↓

Interrupting Someone

When having a conversation, you might occasionally want to interrupt someone. People usually interrupt if they want to ask a question or make a remark while the other person is speaking. Some of the commonly used expressions are listed here. These can be used in formal or informal situations.

Excuse me (for interrupting) but . . .	someone is knocking on my front door.
Pardon me (for interrupting) but . . .	I have to go check the cake in the oven. I think it's burning!
I hate to interrupt but . . .	I have an emergency message for you.
I'm sorry, but . . .	
Can I interrupt a minute?	I think the manager wants us all to leave now.

Changing the Topic of Conversation

When having a conversation, you often want to move the conversation topic in a new direction or completely change it. Some of the commonly used expressions in English are listed here. These can be used in formal and informal situations.

Changing the topic . . .	I saw my old friend, Mike Taylor, yesterday.
That reminds me . . .	
To change the topic . . .	my credit card finally arrived in the mail.
And have you heard that . . .	
Oh, by the way . . .	Alice broke a tooth last weekend.
Oh, before I forget . . .	you're supposed to meet Kevin at 6:00 P.M.

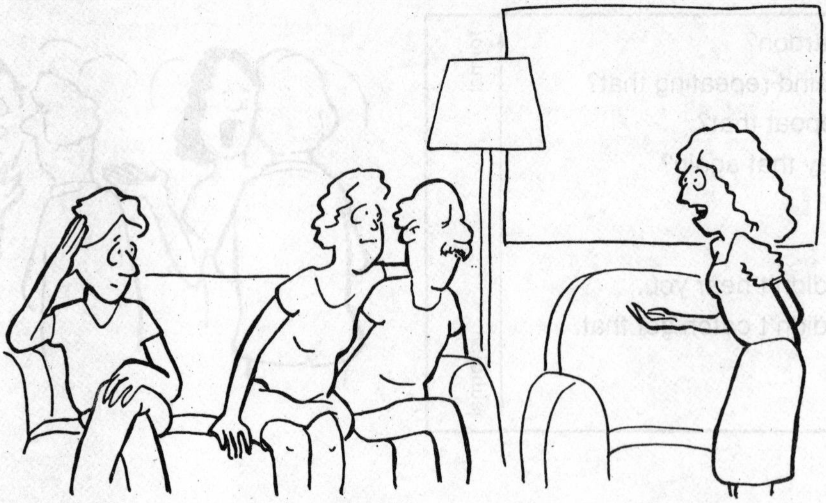

FOR A BETTER UNDERSTANDING

When interrupting someone, you are stopping that person from speaking in the middle of a thought. Normally it is considered most polite to let the other person finish before you begin to speak. For this reason, it's a good idea to interrupt someone only when you have something important to say which can't wait until the other person has finished.

CONVERSATION PRACTICE WITH A FRIEND

1. Find a partner and practice these two conversations aloud.
2. Switch roles for extra practice.

Person A:	I'm broke.* I don't know how I'm going to pay my bills.
Person B:	Oh, that reminds me that your parents called long distance. They want you to call them back. Maybe you could borrow some money from them.

Person A:	I live about ten blocks from here, so I usually just . . .
Person B:	Excuse me for interrupting but my ride is here and I have to go. See you later.
Person A:	See you soon. Goodbye.

* *I'm broke* means *I don't have any money.*

PEOPLE: Two roommates.

INFORMATION TO CONSIDER: The roommates are both men in their early twenties. They are both working and share an apartment together. They have been good friends for several years.

CHANGINC THE TOPIC: One roommate is very depressed. He is broke and doesn't have enough money to pay his bills. That reminds the other roommate that the first roommate's parents called. He suggests that maybe his roommate could borrow some money from his parents.

PEOPLE: Two strangers.

INFORMATION TO CONSIDER: Both people are middle-aged. One is a man; the other is a woman. They are standing outside of a big office building where they both work. They have never met each other before.

INTERRUPTING: The two people are waiting for rides home. The man is making small talk about how he gets home. The woman's ride suddenly arrives. So, she interrupts him, says she has to go, and then says goodbye.

Now You Try It

1. Read the following situations.
2. Find a partner and practice the conversations together.

PEOPLE: A receptionist and a client.

INFORMATION TO CONSIDER: The receptionist is a nineteen-year-old woman. She works for a big publishing company. The client is a middle-aged man. The two people have never met each other.

REPEATING: The client calls and asks to speak to Ms. Baker. Ms. Baker isn't there so the client leaves his phone number and address. The receptionist didn't hear his address correctly so she asks him to repeat the information.

PEOPLE: A husband and wife.

INFORMATION TO CONSIDER: The husband and wife are both in their early thirties. They have a very close, loving relationship.

CHANGING THE TOPIC: The husband and wife are having a conversation at dinner, asking each other about their day. At one point, the husband changes the topic of conversation to tell his wife that he's going to be home late tomorrow night because he has an important meeting at work.

PEOPLE: A customer and a ticket agent.

INFORMATION TO CONSIDER: The customer and the ticket agent are both women. The customer is in her early sixties. The ticket agent is in her early twenties. The two people don't know each other at all. They are talking at the ticket counter.

REPEATING: The customer is asking the ticket agent when the next flight to (city) is leaving. The ticket agent gives the date and time. The customer didn't hear the information and asks the ticket agent to repeat it.

PEOPLE: A salesperson and a customer.

INFORMATION TO CONSIDER: The salesperson is a twenty-five–year old man. The customer is a man in his late fifties. The two people have never met each other before.

REPETITION: The man is at the catalogue department of a department store. He is going to pick up an order he placed from the catalogue. The salesperson asks the customer his name. He says, "I'm Dr. Jaworski." The salesperson doesn't understand the customer. He asks him to repeat his name and then spell it.

PEOPLE: A boss and a secretary.

INFORMATION TO CONSIDER: The boss is a middle-aged man. The secretary is a middle-aged woman. The two people have worked together for several years. They have a professional but friendly relationship.

INTERRUPTING: The boss is talking to one of the other employees. The secretary walks into his office and interrupts the conversation because the business papers he has wanted all morning finally arrived.

PEOPLE: ______________________

____

INFORMATION TO CONSIDER: ______________________

____

____

REPETITION, INTERRUPTING, CHANGING THE TOPIC: ______________________

____

____

____

What Would You Say?

1. You just met a new student in your English class. You ask him his name, but when he tells you, you don't understand. So you say:

   ____

   ____

2. Two of your coworkers are talking out in the hall. One of them just got an important telephone call. You can politely interrupt their conversation by saying:

   ____

   ____

3. Several of your friends are telling ghost and horror stories. All the stories are making you nervous. You politely change the topic of conversation by saying:

   ____

   ____

4. You just called up a local night club and asked the person on the telephone how to get there. The person gave you very complicated directions and you didn't understand what she said. So you say:

   ____

   ____

5. You and several coworkers are talking about a mutual friend who just got engaged. This reminds you that another close friend is getting a divorce and you want to tell everyone before you forget. So, you change the topic by saying:

   ____

   ____

6. You are sitting at a subway stop waiting for the next subway. You notice that a couple near you is arguing about where the nearest pharmacy is. You know where it is located. You very politely interrupt their conversation and tell them where the pharmacy is by saying:

   ____

   ____

7. You are buying a sweater in a big department store. The salesperson tells you how much it costs but you don't understand her. So you ask her:

   ____

   ____

8. You are with a group of friends who are talking very unkindly about a person who isn't there. You'd like to change the topic of conversation as politely and quickly as possible. So you say:

   ____

   ____

9. Your teacher just explained a very important grammar point. You didn't understand it very well. You ask your teacher to repeat what he just said by saying:

____

____

10. It's your first day of classes in a new school. You can't find your classroom. Across the room you see a group of students talking. You walk over to them and politely interrupt to ask for help by saying:

____

____

Rotation Activity

directions:

1. Find a partner. Ask your partner what the best way is to do one of the following actions.
2. Your partner tells you the different steps to complete the action. As he or she tells you the different steps, occasionally interrupt and ask him or her to repeat what was just said. For example:

   Person A: What is the best way to get rid of a cold?

   Person B: Well, you should go to bed and get some rest. Take two aspirin . . .

   Person A: I'm sorry. I didn't hear the last part. Could you say that again?

   Person B: Take two aspirin and drink some tea with honey and lemon.

   Person A: Pardon me, drink some tea with what?

   Person B: With honey and lemon.
3. Here are some actions from which to choose:

   What is the best way to . . .

   A. make a long-distance phone call?
   B. make a tossed salad?
   C. send a package/telegram overseas?
   D. open a savings account?
   E. sew on a button?
   F. get rid of a bad cold?
   G. get rid of a hangover after a big party?
   H. ______________________?
4. Repeat steps one thru three several times with different partners.

Discussion Activity

Find an editorial in a newspaper or magazine about a current event happening internationally, nationally, or locally. Bring your article to class to share with the others.

directions:

1. Divide into groups of three or four people.
2. Have one person in the group present his or her editorial.
3. After, discuss your reactions to the editorial. Do you agree with the article? Do you disagree? Take turns giving your opinions to each other.
4. During your conversation, practice:
   A. Asking someone to repeat what he or she just said.
   B. Interrupting.
   C. Changing the focus of the topic.

Using these speech acts may seem a little artificial at first. But with a little practice, they will become natural and helpful in keeping the conversation going.

COMMUNITY EXERCISES

Briefly describe a problem your city (country) is having:

____

____

____

In your opinion, how should your city (country) solve the problem?

____

____

____

Briefly explain the problem to three other people. Ask them how the city (country) should solve the problem from their point of view. You might want to ask:

In your opinion, how should the city (country) solve this problem?

	first person	*second person*	*third person*
Whose opinion did you ask (a classmate, a stranger, a co-worker)?			
How did you ask the person his or her opinion? Write it here.			
How did the other person reply? Briefly write the reply here.			
Was the situation formal or informal?			

Watch a discussion program on television or attend a discussion at your school or in your community. (If you are unsure, ask your teacher about appropriate television programs. Many programs on Saturday and Sunday mornings have discussion formats with two or more people.) Carefully listen to how people change the flow of conversation throughout the discussion. Then answer the following questions.

1. Where did you watch the discussion? On T.V.? At school? Somewhere in your community? ______________________
2. What was the topic of the discussion? Try to explain in two or three sentences. ______________________
3. Was the discussion formal? Was it relaxed and informal? ______________________
4. How many people were taking part in the discussion? ______________________
5. What expressions did the people use to ask someone to repeat what he or she just said? Did you hear any new expressions? ______________________
6. How often did people ask each other to repeat what they had just said? Frequently? Sometimes? Almost never? ______________________
7. What expressions did people use to interrupt the conversation? Did you hear any new expressions? ______________________
8. Did people ever interrupt each other in a manner that you considered impolite? Explain. ______________________
9. How often did people interrupt each other? Frequently? Sometimes? Almost never? ______________________
10. What expressions did people use to change the topic of conversation or change the focus of the conversation? Did you hear any new expressions? ______________________
11. Did people ever try to change the topic of the conversation in a manner that you considered impolite? Explain. ______________________
12. How often did people try to change the topic or focus of conversation? Frequently? Sometimes? Almost never? ______________________

PUTTING IT TOGETHER

If you've learned this chapter well, you should now be able to: (1) express your opinion; (2) agree with, disagree with, show surprise about someone's opinion; (3) ask someone to repeat himself or herself; (4) interrupt someone speaking; and (5) change the topic of conversation. The following activities give you the opportunity to practice using these skills. You also have a chance to review the information from the other chapters in this book.

Build-Up Role Plays

Create your own role play as a class (or in small groups if the class is large). Use the following directions. Repeat the build-up process to create other role plays.

FIRST PERSON: Choose the functions which you want to use in the role play. Select them from this list:

- Introducing Others or Yourself
- Greetings
- Small Talk Topics
- Invitations
- Apologies
- Condolences
- Expressions of Gratitude
- Compliments, Congratulations
- Requests
- Warnings, Commands, Directions
- Conversation Closings/Goodbyes
- Offering to Do Something
- Seeking Permission
- Advising Someone
- Stating Your Intention to Do Something
- Expressing Pleasure
- Expressing Displeasure
- Expressing Your Opinion
- Asking Someone to Repeat Himself or Herself
- Interrupting Someone Speaking
- Changing the Topic of Conversation

SECOND PERSON: Give a setting for the role play.

THIRD PERSON: Create a role-play situation in that setting, including the players.

FOURTH PERSON: Name the important details to consider to make the role play realistic, including information about the players.

FIFTH, SIXTH, SEVENTH . . . (AS MANY AS NECESSARY) PERSON: Act out the role play.

Mix and Match

1. Column A lists twenty-five statements. Column B lists twenty-five possible replies.
2. Find a partner. Have one person pick a statement from Column A and read it aloud. Then have the other person pick an appropriate reply and read it aloud. (In some cases, there may be more than one appropriate reply.)
3. Continue until you have read all the statements. Switch roles several times.

column a

1. If you ask me, Mr. Peters should go on a diet. He's too fat!
2. Would you like me to help you fix your motorcycle?
3. Excuse me, I didn't hear your last name. Could you repeat it?
4. I don't think we've met. My name is Harold Morton.
5. Would it be possible for me to bring my little brother on the camping trip this weekend?
6. It was so nice being here. I hope I'll see you again sometime.
7. I'm really sorry that I'm late. I overslept again.
8. Would you mind not smoking in my office?
9. I'm getting married tomorrow.
10. Thanks a lot for getting the groceries for me. I really appreciate it.
11. I really enjoy eating hamburgers.
12. Hi (partner's name). How are you doing?
13. Would you like to go to the concert with me?
14. I really like your new stereo! It's fantastic.

column b

a. Me neither. A big dog bit me once.

b. Great! How are you?

c. Thanks a lot. I really like it too.

d. You're kidding! I didn't even know you were engaged.

e. Thank you very much. It was serious, but he's going to be OK in a few weeks.

f. Don't worry about it. We still have plenty of time.

g. You're welcome. I was glad to do it.

h. It's nice to meet you, Mr. Morton. My name is Ken Thompson.

i. It was nice seeing you, too. Goodbye.

j. Sure. My last name is (your name).

k. You're kidding! I think learning a second language is a very valuable experience.

l. See you soon. Take care.

m. I couldn't agree with you more.

n. Thanks anyway, but I just called my mechanic. He's going to fix it.

o. Oh, I'm sorry. I'll put out my cigarette right now.

p. You're right. That's a good idea.

15. I just heard that your brother was in a serious car accident. I'm really sorry.
16. In my opinion, learning a second language is a waste of time.
17. I don't like big dogs. They scare me.
18. Could you repeat the last part? I didn't hear your address.
19. Do you want to go swimming with me this afternoon?
20. Carrie, this is my brother, Bob.
21. It's getting late. I have to go home.
22. I strongly advise you to get a new car before you take that long trip.
23. I'm determined to run in the twenty-six mile marathon next month!
24. Martha, it's so good to see you. It's been such a long time.
25. Can we give Sam a ride home from school?

q. It's nice to meet you, Bob.
r. That's wonderful!
s. You do? I don't. I hate hamburgers.
t. Of course. It would be fun to have your little brother with us.
u. I live at 16 N. 31st Street.
v. It's great to see you, too. How have you been?
w. Sure, I'd love to. That sounds great.
x. I'm afraid not. We don't have enough room in the car.
y. I'm not sure if I can. I'll let you know in an hour.

Sticky Situations

Discuss these situations together.

1. You tell someone that, in your opinion, a particular decision was poorly made. Then you realize that the person to whom you are speaking is the one who made the decision. What should you do?
2. You are talking about something that is very important to you and someone changes the topic. What should you do?